D0911569

FAT MEN
IN SKIRTS

BY NICKY SILVER

★

DRAMATISTS
PLAY SERVICE
INC.

SPECIAL NOTE

Anyone receiving permission to produce FAT MEN IN SKIRTS is required to give credit to the authors as sole and exclusive authors of the play in all programs distributed in connection with performances of the play and in all instances in which the title of the play appears for purposes of advertising, publicizing or otherwise exploiting the play and/or a production thereof; the name of the authors must appear on a separate line, in which no other name appears, immediately beneath the title and in size of type equal to 50% of the largest letter used for the title of the play. No person, firm or entity may receive credit larger than that accorded the authors.

SPECIAL NOTE ON SONGS AND RECORDINGS

For performance of the songs, arrangements and recordings mentioned in this play that are protected by copyright, the permission of the copyright owners must be obtained; or other songs, arrangements and recordings in the public domain substituted.

FAT MEN IN SKIRTS was first presented by The Vortex Theater Company (Robert Coles, Artistic Director), in New York City, under the author's direction in 1988. The production stage manager was Lizze Fitzgerald. The cast was as follows:

PHYLLIS HOGAN .... Stephanie Weatherton
BISHOP HOGAN .... Chuck Coggins
HOWARD HOGAN/DR. NESTOR .... Bill Christ
PAM/POPO MARTIN .... Debra Risen

FAT MEN IN SKIRTS was subsequently produced at The Wooly Mammoth Theater Company in Washington, D.C. (Howard Shalwitz, Artistic Director), on January 10, 1991. It was directed by Howard Shalwitz and Lee Mikeska; the set design was by Keith Belli; the costume design was by Helen Oizhi Huang; the lighting design was by Christopher Townsend; the sound design was by Daniel Schrader; and the production stage manager was Scott Hammer. The cast was as follows:

PHYLLIS HOGAN .... Nancy Robinette
BISHOP HOGAN ....Rob Leo Roy
HOWARD HOGAN/DR. NESTOR .... Grover Gardner
PAM/POPO MARTIN .... Desiree Marie

FAT MEN IN SKIRTS was presented by Naked Angeles Theater Company (Toni Kotite, Artistic Director), in New York City, in March, 1994. It was directed by Joe Mantello; the set design was by Steven Olson; the costume design was by Laura Cunninghan; the lighting design was by Howard Werner; the sound design was by Aural Fixation; the fight choreography was by Rick Sordelet; and the production stage manager was Barnaby Harris. The cast was as follows:

PHYLLIS HOGAN .... Allison Janney
BISHOP HOGAN .... Matt McGrath
HOWARD HOGAN/DR. NESTOR .... Stanley Tucci
PAM/POPO MARTIN .... Marisa Tomei

AUTHOR'S NOTES

FAT MEN IN SKIRTS is, ultimately, a love story, albeit a rather unconventional one. Having been involved in several productions, I have learned that the question of style is paramount. Because there is so much overt humor in the play, I think it is easy to think of it simply as a comedy, or "camp." That is one thing it definitely is not. Of course, it is a comedy, but it must also be frightening. The more ferocious Bishop becomes, the more grounded in genuine panic is the humor. As a guide, I point out that FAT MEN is structured very specifically in three acts. The first act is absurdist and non-linear, in that the action jumps in time and space. The second act is, basically, a one-room farce. The third act is really a court-room drama. The trick is, in performance, to find where these three styles meet, not where they are separate. I would also like to mention that there is much direct address in the play. (Lines preceded by the stage direction "out" are delivered to the audience.) There should be the feeling that these are four people who have come together to tell their story. Each of them is interested in gaining the audience's sympathy — even at each other's expense.

Lastly, I would be remiss if I did not take this space to thank those individuals who helped nurture this play. They include: Chuck Coggins, Stephanie Weatherton, George Lane, Mary Meagher, James Bart Upchurch III, Howard Shalwitz, Bruce Whitacre, Tim Sanford, Nancy Turner and John Hensley, Joe Mantello and John Guare.

CHARACTERS

PHYLLIS HOGAN: An attractive, sophisticated woman in her 40s at the play's opening.

BISHOP HOGAN: Her son. A shy, stuttering little boy of 11 at the play's opening.

HOWARD HOGAN: Her husband. An attractive, womanizing film director.

PAM: A sexy young woman, lacking in logic. Howard's mistress.

DR. NESTOR: A psychiatrist, played by the same actor as Howard.

POPO MARTIN: A mental patient. Dementedly cheery. Played by the same actor as Pam.

TIME AND PLACE

ACT ONE: Five years on a desert island and various locations.

ACT TWO: The Hogan apartment, New York City.

ACT THREE: A hospital for the criminally insane, one year later.

There is one intermission between Acts One and Two.

FAT MEN IN SKIRTS

ACT ONE

In the darkness we hear Bobby Darrin's recording of a song such as "Beyond the Sea."* The lights come up on a beach. There is no foliage, perhaps a lone palm tree. Phyllis Hogan is standing center, with her back to us. She is emptying her shoes of sand. She is clearly overdressed for a day at the beach. She turns and addresses the audience.

PHYLLIS. I loathe the beach. I am Phyllis Hogan and I do so loathe the beach. To me, it is the very definition of monotony. Just sand and water and sand and water. And more sand and more water. Ick. And look, a perfectly good pair of shoes, Susan Bennis/Warren Edwards, crocodile, and completely ruined! I have never understood the appeal of the seashore: sand in your stockings and young girls with better bodies in skimpy swimsuits. When I was a girl I used to bury myself in the sand. Head first.

I've no idea where I am. I was supposed to be in Italy by now, but I've been to Italy, and I always gain weight in Italy, so here I am at the beach. My husband is in Italy, gaining weight no doubt, gorging himself on the local delicacies and the local girls — and perhaps, thinking, only fleetingly, "What could have become of Phyllis?" He's scouting locations for a new film. Something heartwarming about extraterrestrials. I assume. My husband is a filmmaker. He was a director in the seventies, now he's a filmmaker. He makes heartwarming films about lovable extraterrestrials, mostly.

My plane crashed. It's a miracle that I'm alive. I suppose. There were eight of us on the plane, including the pilot.

---

* See Special Note on Songs and Recordings on copyright page.

Only Bishop and I survived. Of course one died of a heart attack during the in-flight movie. It featured Tatum O'Neal. I can't say I was frightened when the plane went down — the film was beastly. I just watched the ground getting closer and closer, spinning around outside my window like a top. I shut my eyes and waited for it to happen: the bang, the crash, the end. And knowing my life was over was kind of a relief in a funny way. The chore of my life was over and I could just relax and wait and see.... But then I opened my eyes and now a perfectly good pair of shoes is down the drain. Damn. You should meet Bishop. Bishop! He's my son. I sent him to go through the pockets of the others. I only have two packs of cigarettes with me and there's no telling how long it'll be before they find us. That was an hour ago. BISHOP! I'll go mad if I don't have some cigarettes. *(Bishop enters from over a dune. He is 11. He's wearing a prep-school uniform. His posture is terrible, hunched over and pigeon-toed. He speaks with a stutter.)*

BISHOP. Yes, M-m-other?

PHYLLIS. What've you been doing?

BISHOP. What did you t-t-tell me t-to do?

PHYLLIS. I told you to go through their pockets for cigarettes.

BISHOP. Well, that's what I've been d-d-doing.

PHYLLIS. And?

BISHOP. Two cigars. *(He offers her two cigars which she takes and puts in her flight bag.)*

PHYLLIS. Thank you. *(Out.)* You never know.

BISHOP. M-m-mother?

PHYLLIS. You needn't address me as "Mother," Bishop. There's no one else alive.

BISHOP. Oh.

PHYLLIS. Well, what is it?

BISHOP. M-m-mother?

PHYLLIS. *(Irritated.)* Yes?

BISHOP. I'm f-f-fr — scared.

PHYLLIS. Of what? We've already crashed.

BISHOP. What will happen t-t-to us?

PHYLLIS. Someone will find us.

8

BISHOP.   B-b-but —

PHYLLIS.   Don't be gloomy. It isn't becoming on little boys.

BISHOP.   B-b-but —

PHYLLIS.   If we'd made it to Italy, you'd be fat by now.

BISHOP.   *(Out.)* Katharine Hepburn made a movie in Italy. *S-s-summertime.* With Rossano B-b-brazzi. It was ad-d-dapted from *The Time of the Cuckoo,* by Arthur Laurents, and later turned into the m-m-musical, *Do I hear a Waltz?* While f-f-filming on the canals of Venice, which are sewers, she fell in and got an eye in-f-fection which caused her to tear all the t-t-time after that.

PHYLLIS.   Very good, Bishop. *(Out.)* Bishop is obsessed with Katharine Hepburn. *(To Bishop.)* Stand up straight.

BISHOP.   *(Out.)* K-k-katharine Hepburn was born November eight, n-n-nineteen-oh-nine. As a young girl, she wore her hair v-v-very short in the summer and was often m-m-mistaken for a boy. She was married to Ludlow Ogden Smith. But only for th-th-th — a little while.

PHYLLIS.   Thank you, Bishop. That will be all about Miss Hepburn.

BISHOP.   Her f-f-first play was *The Art and Mrs. B-b-bottle.*

PHYLLIS.   That will do.

BISHOP.   *(Out.)* Her first film —

PHYLLIS.   That's enough.

BISHOP.   *(Out.)* A *B-b-bill of Divorcement.*

PHYLLIS.   Stop it now.

BISHOP.   *(Out.)* Her f-f-first Oscar was for —

PHYLLIS.   Bishop —

BISHOP.   *(Out.)* M-m-m, was for —

PHYLLIS.   Stop it, Bishop! *(Out.)* Bishop can be quite the little show-off. *(To Bishop.)* No one is interested. No one cares. And if they do, they can buy one of three thousand books currently in print about her.

BISHOP.   Yes, Mother.

PHYLLIS.   Thank you.

BISHOP.   *(Out.) Morning Glory!!*

PHYLLIS.   There's no telling how long we're going to be here, so *please* try to behave.

BISHOP. I'm hungry.

PHYLLIS. Don't think about it.

BISHOP. What should I th-th-think about?

PHYLLIS. Don't you realize how lucky you are to be alive?

BISHOP. No.

PHYLLIS. Well, you are very lucky.

BISHOP. Oh.

PHYLLIS. Everyone else was killed.

BISHOP. I know.

PHYLLIS. They weren't so lucky.

BISHOP. Lucky me.

PHYLLIS. That's right.

BISHOP. I'm l-l-lucky. And I'm hungry.

PHYLLIS. Oh, dig for clams.

BISHOP. I d-d-don't like clams.

PHYLLIS. Have you ever had clams?

BISHOP. No.

PHYLLIS. Then how do you know you don't like them?

BISHOP. They look like snot.

PHYLLIS. Not clams casino.

BISHOP. I'm sorry.

PHYLLIS. You're giving me a headache, Bishop.

BISHOP. I'm sorry.

PHYLLIS. Can't you go play with the dead bodies or something? You're eleven, you should like that sort of thing.

BISHOP. *(Out.)* There were magazines in the cockpit, with p-p-pictures of naked boys doing things to each other.

PHYLLIS. *(Out.)* Probably why we crashed.

BISHOP. I'm hungry.

PHYLLIS. You said that.

BISHOP. I'm s-s-sorry.

PHYLLIS. Try to say new things.

BISHOP. I'm st-t-tarving.

PHYLLIS. Interesting things.

BISHOP. I'm famished.

PHYLLIS. I should be dead now. I tell myself I should be dead or in Italy.

BISHOP. I'm h-h-h —

PHYLLIS.　Bishop!

BISHOP.　Thirsty.

PHYLLIS.　Oh, I'll go look for food. Hold my shoes. They're ruined at this point, but the last thing I need is to lose a heel. *(Phyllis hands Bishop her shoes and exits over the dune. Bishop addresses the audience.)*

BISHOP.　I d-d-didn't mind crashing. Really. It was ek-ek-ek — cool. I'm lucky. We were s-s-spinning and spinning and it was just like being in a movie. K-k-katharine Hepburn played an avi-av-av — lady pilot in the movie *Christopher Strong.* It was never turned into a musical. I am Bishop Hogan. Th-that is my name, I am not a deacon of the church. I'm eleven. My father is famous. He hates Mother. He sleeps with the young girls in his m-m-movies. *(Howard enters from the wings.)*

HOWARD.　*(Out.)* That's not true.

BISHOP.　*(Out.)* He doesn't love my mother and he doesn't love m-m-me.

HOWARD.　*(Out.)* She tells him these things —

BISHOP.　*(Out.)* He's ob-bsessed with his work.

HOWARD.　*(Out.)* To assuage her guilt over a failing marriage and to alienate my son from me.

BISHOP.　*(Out.)* He's self-absorbed.

HOWARD.　*(Out.)* Her words.

BISHOP.　*(Out.)* The only reason I have any friends at all, is b-b-because I give them Arcky dolls.

HOWARD.　*(Out.)* She fills his head with lies.

BISHOP.　*(Out.)* Arcky was the extrat-t-terrestrial in my father's movie.

HOWARD.　They know Arcky. Everybody knows Arcky. Everybody loves him. *(Out.)* They used him in the Pepsi-Cola commercials.

BISHOP.　Why don't you love Mommy?

HOWARD.　*(Out.)* Who said I didn't?

BISHOP.　She did.

HOWARD.　Oh.

BISHOP.　Wh-wh-why?

HOWARD.　She's overbearing.

BISHOP.　What's that?

HOWARD. It's complicated.

PAM. *(Off-stage.)* Hoowwaardd?

BISHOP. Do you think we're d-d-dead?

HOWARD. I haven't thought about it yet.

PAM. *(Off-stage.)* Hoowwwaarrddd!

HOWARD. Excuse me. *(Howard exits. Phyllis enters.)*

PHYLLIS. There is nothing.

BISHOP. Oh?

PHYLLIS. Not so much as a coconut. Oh, give me those, I feel frumpish. This island is a parking lot. *(She takes the shoes.)*

BISHOP. I'm hungry.

PHYLLIS. I know.

BISHOP. Do you think Daddy thinks we're dead?

PHYLLIS. *(Bright.)* Let's talk about sleeping arrangements. Shall we?

BISHOP. I bet he's c-c — worried.

PHYLLIS. It'll be night soon.

BISHOP. He's crying. I bet.

PHYLLIS. Can you build a lean-to?

BISHOP. I miss Daddy.

PHYLLIS. Can you build a lean-to, or a hut, or something?

BISHOP. Do you miss D-d-daddy?

PHYLLIS. Can you, Bishop, build a lean-to?

BISHOP. Of course not.

PHYLLIS. What do you mean, of course not?

BISHOP. I mean I can't.

PHYLLIS. Don't be negative. Why can't you?

BISHOP. Because I can't.

PHYLLIS. That's no attitude. How do you know you can't? You have to try and find out that you can't.

BISHOP. Daddy c-c-could build a lean-to. He could build a split-level twin dwelling.

PHYLLIS. Do not mention your father again tonight.

BISHOP. I'm s-s-sorry. *(Out.)* Katharine Hepburn made *Philadelphia Story* in n-n-n-nineteen-forty-one. After being labeled box-office poison.

PHYLLIS. I'm ignoring that. Now. What will you need to build a lean-to?

BISHOP.   I can't build a lean-to!

PHYLLIS.   Why not?!

BISHOP.   Because I'm hungry!!

PHYLLIS.   Don't raise your voice to me!

BISHOP.   I'm s-s-sorry.

PHYLLIS.   I realize you're frightened —

BISHOP.   I'm hungry —

PHYLLIS.   And hungry.

BISHOP.   You hate me and you wish I was dead.

PHYLLIS.   What a terrible thing to say.

BISHOP.   Why won't you feed me?

PHYLLIS.   Eat seaweed.

BISHOP.   I'm not Chinese.

PHYLLIS.   I thought you were hungry?

BISHOP.   It's poison.

PHYLLIS.   It's sushi.

BISHOP.   It's creepy.

PHYLLIS.   Eat rocks, eat sand — oh, hand me my purse. *(He does so.)* Here. Eat lipstick. It's not poison.

BISHOP.   Thank you. *(He eats it.)*

PHYLLIS.   *(Out.)* He was always a picky eater. As a baby, Bishop threw up everything five minutes after he ate it. Tell you the truth, I thought he was bulimic.

BISHOP.   Done!

PHYLLIS.   You didn't save me any?

BISHOP.   I didn't think you l-l-liked lipstick.

PHYLLIS.   That's not the point.

BISHOP.   I'm sorry.

PHYLLIS.   *(Bright.)* Now. What will you need to build a lean-to?

BISHOP.   M-m-mother?

PHYLLIS.   You can get supplies from the wreckage —

BISHOP.   M-m-mother?

PHYLLIS.   You can build here, with a southern exposure and a view of the sea —

BISHOP.   M-m-mother!

PHYLLIS.   That'll be lovely —

BISHOP.   Mommy!

PHYLLIS.   What is it?

BISHOP.   I'm still hungry.

PHYLLIS.   You just ate a whole lipstick.

BISHOP.   We're going to starve to death, aren't we?

PHYLLIS.   Don't be ridiculous. I have lots of lipsticks. *(Out.)* Different colors for different outfits.

BISHOP.   You can't live on lipstick.

PHYLLIS.   I don't see why not.

BISHOP.   It has no v-v-vitamins.

PHYLLIS.   We'll fish.

BISHOP.   We have no t-t-tackle.

PHYLLIS.   We'll hunt.

BISHOP.   We're going to starve to death!!

PHYLLIS.   We'll trim down!

BISHOP.   I'm thin now!

PHYLLIS.   Five pounds, and you'll be amazed at how clothing hangs off of you!

BISHOP.   You don't care.

PHYLLIS.   Please, I'm tired, I'm irritated and I have sand in my stockings! Try to cooperate. Now, if the lean-to faces this way, the morning sun will get in my eyes —

BISHOP.   WE'RE GOING TO DIE! I DON'T WANT TO DIE! WE'RE GOING TO STARVE TO DEATH!! WE'LL DIE!!

PHYLLIS.   ALL RIGHT!! All right. Hand me my purse. *(He does so. She pulls out a huge butcher's knife.)* Here's a knife. Now. Go back to the plane and cut the arm off that nun. Bring it back here and I'll cook it and we'll eat it.

BISHOP.   What?

PHYLLIS.   Go cut off the nun's arm and I'll cook it. All right?

BISHOP.   I c-c-can't!

PHYLLIS.   Pardon me?

BISHOP.   I c-c-can't do that.

PHYLLIS.   I thought you were hungry. I'm sorry.

BISHOP.   I am.

PHYLLIS.   Do you think it's going to start raining cheeseburgers?

BISHOP.   N-n-no.

PHYLLIS.   Can you eat the air? Can you eat the water?

BISHOP. N-n-no.

PHYLLIS. So what are you going to eat?

BISHOP. I don't know!

PHYLLIS. Do you want to starve to death?

BISHOP. I can't d-d-do it!!

PHYLLIS. Look! I'm frightened too! Don't you think I'm scared? I am. I'm scared. So what? What do we do? Do we sit here and watch each other decay? Quizzing each other on Katharine Hepburn trivia while we wither to skeletons? Is that it? Or do we take matters into our own hands? She's already dead. You're not doing anything wrong.

BISHOP. *(Out.)* She was a nun!

PHYLLIS. That's why I picked her!

BISHOP. Don't m-m-make me.

PHYLLIS. It's time to grow up.

BISHOP. Why don't you love me?

PHYLLIS. Who said I don't?

BISHOP. If you loved me you w-wouldn't make me d-d-do this.

PHYLLIS. No. I'd let you starve to death. In front of me. I'd let you die. That, I take it, would be proof of my maternal instincts.

BISHOP. You do it.

PHYLLIS. Let's be realistic. You are wearing Dalton blues. I have on my Michael Kors.

BISHOP. What's that?

PHYLLIS. My dress, which I'd just as soon not splatter with blood.

BISHOP. I c-c-can't.

PHYLLIS. It's easy.

BISHOP. I'm not hungry anymore.

PHYLLIS. Just do it!

BISHOP. Lipstick filled me up. That was one big lipstick.

PHYLLIS. Make me proud? Please, Bishop.

BISHOP. But —

PHYLLIS. *(Gentle.)* When you get back, we'll build a fire.

BISHOP. Yes, M-m-mother.

PHYLLIS. That's a good boy. *(Bishop exits over a dune. Phyllis addresses the audience.)* I had a child whom I loved and whom I taught to sever the arms of nuns. *(There is a light change, indicating a flashback. Howard enters, perhaps wearing tails. Phyllis may drop some piece of her costume. She joins him. It is their wedding night. She is giddy and young.)*

HOWARD.   Are you happy?

PHYLLIS.   It was a beautiful wedding.

HOWARD.   It was.

PHYLLIS.   Canary and avocado.

HOWARD.   You were a beautiful bride.

PHYLLIS.   Do you love me, Howard?

HOWARD.   I do, dumpling.

PHYLLIS.   My name is Phyllis.

HOWARD.   I know that.

PHYLLIS.   Why did you call me dumpling?

HOWARD.   It was a euphemism.

PHYLLIS.   *(As if he'd sneezed.)* God bless you. *(Out.)* I was young and used to coasting on my looks.

HOWARD.   You look very beautiful, there by the window.

PHYLLIS.   Me? You mean me?

HOWARD.   *(Out.)* She was silly. She was a breath of fresh air. *(To Phyllis.)* Let's go to bed.

PHYLLIS.   Are you sleepy?

HOWARD.   That's not what I meant, Sweetpea.

PHYLLIS.   Sweetpea? Who's Sweetpea?

HOWARD.   That's not what I meant.

PHYLLIS.   What did you mean? By what? When? Where were we?

HOWARD.   Let's make love.

PHYLLIS.   Couldn't we get to know each other first?

HOWARD.   It's our wedding night.

PHYLLIS.   It's never too late.

HOWARD.   Come to bed.

PHYLLIS.   My sister Marie, who was always the smart one, says that sex is a beautiful, special event, and a woman's only real power over a man.

HOWARD.   You have a beautiful neck.

PHYLLIS.   My mother says "What will you have and how

would you like that cooked?" She's a waitress.

HOWARD. Beautiful ears.

PHYLLIS. My father just grunts if you block the TV.

HOWARD. Beautiful lips.

PHYLLIS. *(Out.)* He has remote control. He likes wrestling.

HOWARD. Beautiful shoulders.

PHYLLIS. I want a baby.

HOWARD. Why?

PHYLLIS. You would like me better if I had a baby.

HOWARD. I don't know if that's true, cookiepuss.

PHYLLIS. *(Frustrated.)* I keep telling you —

HOWARD. I know, I know. Your name is Phyllis.

PHYLLIS. I think if we had a child we would be bonded. And you would feel, even if only unconsciously, a debt of gratitude towards me for supplying you with a miniature version of yourself, who would in turn reproduce and continue the cycle, ensuring, in an abstract way, your immortality, thus easing your fear of death.

HOWARD. Phyllis?

PHYLLIS. I read it.

HOWARD. Let's go to bed.

PHYLLIS. I want to make a baby!

HOWARD. I want to hold you. I want to protect you. I want to keep you with me forever and shield you from the world. I want to take care of you.

PHYLLIS. I think I'd like that.

HOWARD. You would, cupcake.

PHYLLIS. My name is —

HOWARD. Stop talking. *(Howard embraces her and kisses her. Bishop appears, standing atop the dune. He holds high the nun's arm, dripping with blood, still clutching a rosary.)*

BISHOP. I DID IT!!! *(Phyllis and Howard look up at Bishop. There is a blackout. Phyllis walks into a pool of light and addresses the audience.)*

PHYLLIS. Lately, I have been having a recurring dream. When I was a little girl, we lived in a part of Philadelphia called Society Hill. In an apartment. Down the hall from us lived a Mr. Antonelli. Mr. Antonelli worked at the Museum of

Natural History. And he was big. He was a big man. Must've weighed three hundred pounds. He was the fattest human being I'd ever seen, close up. But he was well-groomed. And on certain nights of the week, Saturdays, I think, Saturdays mostly and Thursdays, Mr. Antonelli would dress as a woman and go wherever three-hundred-pound men who dress as women go, to seek whatever they can mistake for love. He'd put on a skirt and a blouse, sometimes a mumu-Bloody-Mary-type thing. And a lot of makeup. He wore a wig, a reddish kind of Ethel Merman affair. And always lovely matching jewelry sets: green rhinestone earrings, green rhinestone bracelets, brooches. He got all dolled up and went off to seek others like himself (although I can't imagine there were many others like Mr. Antonelli; three-hundred-pound transvestites are pretty much on their own in the world, I should think). When I was six, I was going to a friend's birthday party one Saturday, and I was wearing the sweetest little powder-blue jumper, and Mr. Antonelli got into the elevator with my mother and me. He looked down at me — this great mountain of gelatinous white flesh, and said, "My goodness, what a sweet little blue dress you have on." And I said, "You could borrow it sometime, if you want, Mr. Antonelli." I was six, and the concept of Junior and Misses sizing had not yet been made clear to me. Well, my mother squeezed my hand so tightly I thought my fingers would snap off. Once on the street, she explained to me that I must never, ever speak to Mr. Antonelli again. If he spoke to me, I was to nod politely. But I was never — under any circumstances — to speak to him again. And I was certainly not to get into the elevator with him. My mother explained to me that Mr. Antonelli was a freak. That he should be locked up. Forgotten about. That Mr. Antonelli, although not to blame him for his condition, was nevertheless, the lowest form of the species, a creature to fear, and his parents, poor souls, must have a terrible burden to bear.

Now. In my dream, I'm a little girl again. And I'm wearing my little powder-blue jumper. The one I wore that day. Only,

I'm not on my way to any birthday party. I'm on a field trip with my class from school. We're at the zoo. Riding the monorail and laughing. The sun is shining, balloons fill the sky and we have cotton candy for lunch. We go to the reptile house and the polar-bear cage and the tigers are sunning themselves. Then we go to the monkey house. But there aren't any monkeys. There are, climbing the jungle gym, picking salt from their hair, dozens and dozens of fat men in skirts. Huge fat men, with matching jewelry sets, swinging from limb to limb, laughing in no language. And everyone laughs and points. And then they turn around. All the monkeys. All the men, turn around at once. They turn around and look at me, right at me. And they all have the same face. And it's Bishop's face. They all have my son's face. *(Bishop steps into the light, holding a trousered leg.)* Who's for dinner?

BISHOP.   Leg of pilot. *(Phyllis takes the leg. Exits. Out.)* My father has a mistress. I think he always has. *(The lights come up on Howard and Pam.)*

HOWARD.   I think I could love you.

PAM.   Well, thanks.

HOWARD.   What did you say your name was again?

PAM.   I didn't.

HOWARD.   You have beautiful legs.

PAM.   It's Pam. Pamela. Pam.

HOWARD.   It's a beautiful name. Would you like something to eat?

PAM.   No thank you.

HOWARD.   Are you sure?

PAM.   I don't eat.

HOWARD.   I don't understand.

PAM.   I take liquid protein.

HOWARD.   Oh?

PAM.   And amphetamines.

HOWARD.   Don't you get hungry?

PAM.   I fill up on pills.

HOWARD.   You look thin to me.

PAM.   *(Out.)* The camera adds ten pounds.

HOWARD.   You're an actress?

PAM.   Yes. Maybe you've seen some of my films? *Hannah Does Her Sisters, Lubricating Rita, Fatal Erection, True Clit, Star Whores, Anal Weapon, A Room with a View?*

HOWARD.   You were in *A Room with a View?*

PAM.   No. I just said that. I don't know why.

HOWARD.   Oh. I direct films.

PAM.   I know that. I've seen every one of your movies.

HOWARD.   Really?

PAM.   No.

HOWARD.   Oh. Would you like a drink?

PAM.   No. I don't drink.

HOWARD.   Why not?

PAM.   I gave it up.

HOWARD.   When?

PAM.   I drink. I don't know why I said that.

HOWARD.   Well, would you like one?

PAM.   Yes. No.

HOWARD.   Are you nervous?

PAM.   Yes. Not really. I took a Dietack at three o'clock.

HOWARD.   You look thin to me —

PAM.   *(Out.)* The camera adds ten pounds —

HOWARD.   Should we go to bed?

PAM.   That's very direct.

HOWARD.   I'm sorry.

PAM.   *(Out.)* I like that in a man.

HOWARD.   Do you?

PAM.   *(Out.)* No. Of course not. All day on the set, that's what I get. Nice to meet you. Roll tape and penetration.

HOWARD.   Would you like to go?

PAM.   I think so.

HOWARD.   I'll get your coat.

PAM.   I mean I want to stay. I find you incredibly attractive. I think you might be the handsomest man I've ever seen.

HOWARD.   Really?

PAM.   Of course not. I mean you're nice-looking, but I just said that. I thought you'd like to hear it. I guess. I mean I do think you're fine. Is your penis big?

HOWARD.   Yes.

PAM. Really?

HOWARD. No. I mean I guess it's average.

PAM. It doesn't matter.

HOWARD. Really?

PAM. *(Out.)* To some people.

HOWARD. It matters to you?

PAM. No.

HOWARD. Good.

PAM. *(Out.)* It matters.

HOWARD. Yes?

PAM. No.

HOWARD. Good.

PAM. You direct movies?

HOWARD. Yes.

PAM. You could put me in one.

HOWARD. I could.

PAM. Would you?

HOWARD. Yes.

PAM. Really?

HOWARD. No. I just said that hoping it would make you more eager to have sex with me and less concerned about my genital size.

PAM. I see. Your bluntness verges on insulting.

HOWARD. That's the way I am. Abrupt and self-absorbed.

PAM. I find it repulsive.

HOWARD. We're attracted to that which repels us.

PAM. Oh?

HOWARD. I hope so. My marriage is based on it.

PAM. I think I should go.

HOWARD. That might be best.

PAM. It was nice meeting you.

HOWARD. I'll get you a cab. *(They embrace and sink to the ground. Bishop enters a pool of light and addresses the audience.)*

BISHOP. Katharine Hepburn made *Suddenly Last Summer* in n-n-nineteen-fifty-nine. It was based on a one-act play by Tennessee Williams. B-b-both she, and Elizabeth Taylor were n-n-nominated for Oscars for the film. It is the story of Violet Venable, Katharine Hepburn's efforts to have her n-n-niece,

Elizabeth Taylor, lobotomized by Doctor Montgomery Clift. She wants to stop Liz from telling the world about her son, Sebastian — named for St. Sebastian, who was pecked to death by crows, like Tippi Hedren in the movie, *The Birds*. *(His stutter is gone.)* It seems, Sebastian was this homo who used to use Katharine to lure young men on tropical islands, until she got too old and he had to use Liz. (And Katharine had the hots for junior herself, sorta.) But last summer he was eaten to death by homo-cannibals, which according to the movie had something to do with sea turtles and Elizabeth Taylor's bathing suit becoming transparent when it got wet. *(He looks at his feet, which straighten themselves from their pigeon-toed stance.)* According to legend, and her biography, by Charles Higham, Katharine Hepburn had to have homosexuality explained to her by Joseph Mankiewicz. Now, I don't think it's possible to have worked in Hollywood for twenty-five years and not to have figured it out. I think anyone who claims not to know that kind of thing is hiding something because they're nervous. I think this probably relates to why Katharine Hepburn only lived with her husband, Ludlow Ogden Smith for a few months, but had the same secretary, Laura Harding, for over twenty years. *(He takes a moment and stands up perfectly straight, for the first time.)* Anyway, in the end of the movie, Monty saves Liz and Katharine loses her marbles. It was in black and white. *(His voice drops to a deeper register. He now speaks strongly, coldly.)* I do not mind it on the island. The sky is almost always blue. I can do what I want. I can be by myself. It was not like that at home. *(Lights come up on Phyllis, young and silly, holding a baby, and Howard, reading. Bishop watches.)*

PHYLLIS.   He's a beautiful baby. Marie says he's beautiful. My mother says we're out of mashed potatoes and did you want dessert?

HOWARD.   Uh-huh.

BISHOP.   *(Out.)* I can't remember this.

PHYLLIS.   I think he looks like you.

BISHOP.   But I do.

PHYLLIS.   Except he doesn't have any hair. If we shaved

your head he'd look more like you. Or we could get him a little wig. Do you think we could get him a little wig, Howard? Would you like a little Zsa Zsa Gabor synthetic wig, Baby?

HOWARD. I'm reading.

BISHOP. Look at me.

PHYLLIS. Look at him Howard.

HOWARD. I'm reading.

BISHOP. Look at me.

PHYLLIS. We should name him Howard — I don't mean we should name him Howard — although we could — I mean, Howard, we should name him.

BISHOP. *(To Phyllis.)* Don't name me Howard.

HOWARD. Not now, I'm reading.

PHYLLIS. But it's been two months!

BISHOP. *(To Howard.)* I need a name.

HOWARD. Darling —

PHYLLIS. Who?

HOWARD. Phyllis —

PHYLLIS. What?

HOWARD. You're in my light.

PHYLLIS. We can't keep calling him Baby. It's embarrassing —

HOWARD. Can't you see that I'm reading?

BISHOP. *(To Howard.)* So what?

PHYLLIS. I'm sorry.

HOWARD. I have to read now.

PHYLLIS. What are you reading?

HOWARD. A book.

PHYLLIS. But Howard —

HOWARD. You're in my light.

PHYLLIS. I'm sorry.

HOWARD. Thank you.

PHYLLIS. I suppose we could call him Baby.

HOWARD. Uh-huh.

PHYLLIS. Baby Hogan. It has a ring. No, no. I don't like it. The other children will make fun of him.

HOWARD. He doesn't know any other children.

PHYLLIS. But he will.

BISHOP.   *(Out.)* Not really.

PHYLLIS.   And I don't think Baby is an appropriate name. What if he's tall? People will say, "Here comes that big Baby."

HOWARD.   *(Out.)* This went on for months.

PHYLLIS.   I'll name you baby. I don't mean I'll name you Baby, I mean baby, I'll name you.

HOWARD.   *(Out.)* What was sweet became cloying.

PHYLLIS.   That's kind of jazzy.

HOWARD.   *(Out.)* What was charming became grating.

PHYLLIS.   You're pink. We'll call you Pink Hogan — no, no, that's faggy.

HOWARD.   *(Out.)* What was endearing became insufferable.

PHYLLIS.   Blue. Blue is for boys — no, no. People will think you were a blue baby.

HOWARD.   *(Out.)* I worked more and more.

PHYLLIS.   What do you think Howard, do you like pink or blue?

HOWARD.   I like brown.

PHYLLIS.   For a name?

HOWARD.   As a color.

PHYLLIS.   We can't call him brown, Howard. People will think we're Negroes.

HOWARD.   Please stop talking.

BISHOP.   Name me!

PHYLLIS.   We have to name the baby, Howard.

BISHOP.   Name me!

PHYLLIS.   We have to! It's humiliating! The other mothers come up to me in the supermarket and they say, "Oooo what an adorable baby, what's his name?"

HOWARD.   *(Out.)* It's like living with a metronome!

PHYLLIS.   And I just say the first thing that comes into my head! The other day he was Cap'n Crunch — I was in cereal.

HOWARD.   *(Snapping.)* WHAT AM I DOING!?

PHYLLIS.   What?

HOWARD.   WHAT AM I DOING?

PHYLLIS.   Reading?

HOWARD.   THAT'S RIGHT! THAT'S RIGHT!

PHYLLIS.   Don't yell at me! *(To Bishop.)* Hold this. *(She hands*

Bishop the baby.) Don't yell at me!

HOWARD.   YOU CAN SEE THAT I'M READING!

PHYLLIS.   You don't love me anymore!

HOWARD.   What are you talking about?

PHYLLIS.   You never used to yell at me!

HOWARD.   You never used to get on my nerves —

PHYLLIS.   I get on your nerves?!!!

HOWARD.   Just a little — *(Out.)* All the time. *(To Phyllis.)* Now and then.

PHYLLIS.   You used to think I was funny! Now you think I'm stupid!

HOWARD.   No I don't. *(Out.)* Like a post. *(To Phyllis.)* Not at all.

PHYLLIS.   I know you do! I see you roll your eyes when I ask you questions — you used to be flattered, now you're annoyed!

HOWARD.   Calm down.

PHYLLIS.   But how will I learn if I don't ask questions?! A person has to ask questions! I can change! You'll see! I can get smarter! I can get more sophisticated! GIMMEE THAT BOOK! What's it about? *(Phyllis grabs the book and exits.)*

BISHOP.   *(Looking at the baby.)* I am an adorable baby. *(Pam enters and addresses the audience.)*

PAM.   Howard loves me. I am a hundred percent secure in that. We make love every day and it's beautiful and he holds me next to himself and he whispers my name over and over again and I hear music and I make him do things he doesn't know he wants to. Well maybe not every day. But Howard is a wonderful lover, and I'm in a position to know. I started when I was twelve, with a cousin-by-marriage. And I have had hundreds of lovers since — both in front of the camera and behind, if you know what I mean. But the fact of the matter is, I never felt anything before Howard. Oh sure, I felt things, other things, but not the thing I thought I was supposed to feel. And yes! I know he's married, and he can't let go. But listen. This is my life and my future and my old age around the bend and I can't worry about who I'm hurting, because everybody has to take responsibility for their own actions. *(Pam exits. Lights come up on Bishop eating the baby which had been him in the last scene.)*

BISHOP. *(Out.)* There was a baby on the plane. *(Phyllis enters, weak, weary and disheveled. She drags a bloody, trousered leg.)*

PHYLLIS. Bishop?

BISHOP. What?

PHYLLIS. You're eating the baby.

BISHOP. So?

PHYLLIS. I thought we were saving the baby.

BISHOP. For what?

PHYLLIS. Dessert.

BISHOP. Well, I'm eating it.

PHYLLIS. I wish we had more lipsticks.

BISHOP. For snacks?

PHYLLIS. For my lips. I feel frumpish.

BISHOP. You look fine. You look the same.

PHYLLIS. I can't go on.

BISHOP. Don't be negative.

PHYLLIS. The lean-to is a pigsty.

BISHOP. Don't whine.

PHYLLIS. Was it a boy or a girl?

BISHOP. Boy.

PHYLLIS. Was he cute?

BISHOP. I didn't notice.

PHYLLIS. He cried on the plane.

BISHOP. You can't remember that.

PHYLLIS. I do.

BISHOP. It was months ago.

PHYLLIS. Was it?

BISHOP. Or years.

PHYLLIS. But I remember. He cried on the plane. I guess the air pressure bothered him, made his ears pop.

BISHOP. Don't think about it.

PHYLLIS. He cried and cried and his mother tried to get him to stop but she couldn't. And I kept thinking they should just put him in the overhead baggage compartment.

BISHOP. You don't remember it. You think you do.

PHYLLIS. And now you're eating him. It.

26

BISHOP. It's good.

PHYLLIS. Is it?

BISHOP. Tender. You want some?

PHYLLIS. No thanks. I have a leg.

BISHOP. Baby's better.

PHYLLIS. Would you know it if I lost my mind?

BISHOP. I'd know it.

PHYLLIS. I think I've lost my mind.

BISHOP. You haven't. You were always queer.

PHYLLIS. But my hands look unfamiliar to me.

BISHOP. You need a manicure.

PHYLLIS. True. But it's more than that.

BISHOP. Let me see. *(She shows him her hands.)* They're your hands. That's them.

PHYLLIS. What if you lost your mind, too? What if we're two loons, nutty as fruitcakes and there's no one else around as a sanity barometer.

BISHOP. I haven't.

PHYLLIS. I can't hear you stutter anymore.

BISHOP. I don't stutter anymore.

PHYLLIS. You don't?

BISHOP. No.

PHYLLIS. When did that happen?

BISHOP. Months ago.

PHYLLIS. I didn't hear it go away.

BISHOP. It was gradual.

PHYLLIS. *(After a long pause.)* I see things. I look up at the sky and the clouds arrange themselves into hot-air balloons. Beautiful balloons, all different colors, like a box of crayons. And they block the sun. And I'm in one, and I fly away.

BISHOP. *(Sadistic.)* Katharine Hepburn played —

PHYLLIS. *(Terrified.)* No.

BISHOP. A hot-air balloonist —

PHYLLIS. No, no. Please —

BISHOP. In *Olly Olly Oxenfree!*

PHYLLIS. No!

BISHOP. She did her own stunts!

PHYLLIS. I don't want to hear it! I don't want to hear

about it!

BISHOP. She flew the balloon herself!

PHYLLIS. NO! NO! NO MORE ABOUT HER!

BISHOP. It was directed by Richard Colla!!

PHYLLIS. PLEASE, BISHOP, PLEASE!

BISHOP. IT WAS NEVER RELEASED!!

PHYLLIS. STOP IT STOP IT!!

BISHOP. IT WAS SOLD DIRECTLY TO HBO!!

PHYLLIS. I AM YOUR MOTHER!!

BISHOP. SO WHAT?

PHYLLIS. I FORBID IT!

BISHOP. Forbid what?

PHYLLIS. PLEASE!!

BISHOP. What do you forbid? WHAT?

PHYLLIS. LEAVE ME ALONE!

BISHOP. SAY IT!

PHYLLIS. No, don't make me!

BISHOP. SAY! IT!!

PHYLLIS. YOU MAY NOT —

BISHOP. I MAY NOT?!

PHYLLIS. MAY NOT MENTION —

BISHOP. WHO?!

PHYLLIS. HER!!

BISHOP. WHO!!?

PHYLLIS. YOU KNOW WHO!

BISHOP. Who do you mean? I'm not sure I understand.

PHYLLIS. YOU KNOW WHO I MEAN!!

BISHOP. SAY IT!! SAY IT!! GOD DAMN YOU!!

PHYLLIS. *(In a wild frenzy, she tries to begin the play again.)* Iloaththe beach. IamPhyllisHoganandIdosoloaththebeach. Itistheverydefinitionofmonotony. Justsandandwaterandsandandwaterandmoresandandmorewater. Andlookaperfectlygoodpairofshoes. SusanBennis/WarrenEdwardscrocodileandcompletelyruinedI'veneverunder —

BISHOP. SAY IT!

PHYLLIS. Iloaththe beach/Iloaththe beach/Iloaththe beach —

BISHOP. WHO CAN'T I MENTION!! WHO! SAY IT!!

28

PHYLLIS.   KATHARINE HEPBURN!!!!

BISHOP.   WHO!!!??

PHYLLIS.   KATHARINE HEPBURN! KATHARINE HEP-
BURN!! KA-THA-RINE-HEP-BURN!! THERE! I FORBID YOU!!
I FORBID IT! YOU WILL NOT SAY HER NAME AGAIN!!!

BISHOP.   Who, Mother?

PHYLLIS.   KA! THA! RINE! HEP! BURN! KATHARINE-
HEPBURN!!

BISHOP.   HA HA HA HAAAA!

PHYLLIS.   I hate you, I hate you, I hate you, I — *(She rushes
off-stage.)*

BISHOP.   It's so easy to get under her skin. *(Bishop sits and
eats "the baby." Pam enters, followed by Howard. She takes a pill.)*

HOWARD.   I wish you'd stop.

PAM.   I wish I was the Queen of France.

HOWARD.   I thought, if you were happy, you would stop.

PAM.   If I were to stop, I wouldn't be happy.

HOWARD.   Aren't you happy?

PAM.   Yes. No.

HOWARD.   Don't I make you happy?

PAM.   It's not that simple.

HOWARD.   Of course it is.

PAM.   Leave me alone.

HOWARD.   I want you to stop taking pills.

PAM.   You're not my father.

HOWARD.   Please.

PAM.   What do you care?

HOWARD.   I don't know, maybe it's me. But I'd just as
soon not have you shriek in the night that your feet are gone
and the walls are laughing at you.

PAM.   My feet were laughing at me and the walls flew away.
You are so self-absorbed.

HOWARD.   I'd rather not have to worry, when we go
through customs, that they'll find LSD in your *Harper's Bazaar.*

PAM.   Well they didn't, did they?

HOWARD.   That isn't the point.

PAM.   No. The point is, it was *House and Garden.*

HOWARD.   How can that be the point?

PAM. It is. It is exactly the point. Because you're so wrapped up in yourself you don't even know if I'm smuggling stuff in *Harper's Bazaar* or *House and Garden* when the two magazines are completely different. They have absolutely nothing in common.

HOWARD. *(Out.)* They're both magazines.

PAM. Have you ever read *Harper's Bazaar?* I don't think so. I don't think you could have or you couldn't confuse it with *House and Garden*. *House and Garden* is just pictures of rich people's homes and decorating ideas. *Harper's Bazaar* is fashion and gossip and much trendier. But it doesn't relate to you, so you wouldn't know that.

HOWARD. What's that got to do with your drug problem?

PAM. I don't have a drug problem.

HOWARD. I think you do.

PAM. It's strictly recreational.

HOWARD. You are continually stoned.

PAM. I have a lot of free time.

HOWARD. What do you want?

PAM. Marry me.

HOWARD. Stop and I'll marry you.

PAM. Marry me and I'll stop.

HOWARD. You go first.

PAM. You go first.

HOWARD. You go first.

PAM. You go first.

HOWARD. You go first.

PAM. They're not coming back.

HOWARD. I don't want to talk about it.

PAM. It's been three years.

HOWARD. Let's go to bed.

PAM. They're dead, Howard. They are.

HOWARD. You don't understand.

PAM. Marry me, Howard.

HOWARD. No.

PAM. I think we should separate.

HOWARD. Maybe you're right.

PAM. I think maybe it's time.

HOWARD.   I think maybe we should.

PAM.   I think you should move out.

HOWARD.   I think maybe I ought to.

PAM.   I think that would be best.

HOWARD.   I think maybe you're right. *(They embrace. Bishop steps forward into a pool of light. He addresses the audience. He is now a frightening, feral beast, rhythmic, ruthless and savage in his manner.)*

BISHOP.   My body is like this building, that I'm building one brick at a time. One brick at a fucking time. There is life on the island. The monkeys have come outta the trees. There are maggots on the rotting branches and a fistful makes lunch. There are birds in the sky and I can hit them with rocks and we eat them. I'm not afraid of the animals. They're afraid of me, brilliant mutherfuckers. My body is a weapon. And my stomach feels good against my hands. And my face and my legs and my dick are made of concrete. And I can run faster than the monkeys and I can catch the fish with my metal hands. And there are wild dogs with open sores and monkeys fucking all around us in the night. I watch 'em. And they hump each other like crazy wild animals, screaming, crying, making fucking monkey sounds and twisting like epileptics tied up with rope. And I watch 'em. And they pound each other, hard, like parents. And I watch 'em. And they foam at the mouth and their eyes roll back in their heads. And I watch 'em and I pull my stone dick with my metal hands. And their ape arms flail away like insects in water. And I hold my breath so they don't hear me. And I stay in the dark so they don't see me. And they cry like fucking monkey bastards, shrill shrieking fire and help in monkey tongues. And I pull harder my concrete joint with my manmade hands and they don't even know I'm there! AND I SHOOT MY SHIT INTO THE AIR AND I SCREAM, "YAAHHHHH!! YAHHHHH! YAHHHH!" AND THE DUMB FUCKING MONKEY BASTARDS DON'T KNOW WHAT THE FUCK'S GOING ON! AND THEY DON'T KNOW WHAT THE FUCK I AM! AND THEY SCREAM BACK STUPID FUCKING MONKEY SOUNDS AND RUN AND I LAY BACK AND LAUGH. THE

STUPID FUCKING MONKEY BASTARDS!! *(Phyllis and Howard enter. Bishop's rage is echoed by Phyllis.)*

PHYLLIS.   Howard!

HOWARD.   Phyllis?

BISHOP.   *(Now referring to Phyllis, Howard.)* Stupid fucking bastards!

PHYLLIS.   There's someone else, isn't there?

HOWARD.   No.

BISHOP.   Liars!

PHYLLIS.   Don't lie to me!

HOWARD.   All right.

PHYLLIS.   There is, isn't there?

HOWARD.   *(Out.)* I don't want to hurt her.

PHYLLIS.   I hate dishonesty.

HOWARD.   *(Out.)* I hate scenes.

PHYLLIS.   I hate lies!

HOWARD.   *(Out.)* I hate confrontations.

PHYLLIS.   I hate my life.

HOWARD.   I love you.

PHYLLIS.   Do you? Do you really?

HOWARD.   You mean right now? Right at this moment in time?

PHYLLIS.   Yes!

HOWARD.   *(Going to her.)* Phyllis —

PHYLLIS.   *(Breaking away.)* Don't touch me!

HOWARD.   We have to talk.

PHYLLIS.   I DON'T WANT TO TALK! What do you want Howard? Do you have the vaguest idea!? You didn't want me stupid, and you don't want me smart! Well tell me what you do want! Tell me what new permutation you want this year! I can do it Howard! I can make myself again and again and again! Only be careful, because I will!

HOWARD.   What are you talking about?

PHYLLIS.   Do you even remember what I was? Do you? When you thought you wanted someone nice? When I was nice! Because I was!

HOWARD.   No. I don't remember that at all.

PHYLLIS.   Do you want me to be hurt? Do you want me to

retaliate?

HOWARD.   I want you to be happy!

PHYLLIS.   WHO IS IT!!?

HOWARD.   It's no one.

PHYLLIS.   No one in particular? You mean it's many?

HOWARD.   Let's go away.

PHYLLIS.   For what?

HOWARD.   Try again.

PHYLLIS.   *(Arch.)* The irony is, I think I stopped loving you a long time ago. But I didn't notice. And I was faithful because I was busy. And I never noticed how little I cared.

HOWARD.   People make mistakes.

PHYLLIS.   They certainly do.

HOWARD.   I'm sorry.

PHYLLIS.   Contrition becomes you.

HOWARD.   I have to go to Italy.

PHYLLIS.   Enjoy the pasta.

HOWARD.   Join me?

PHYLLIS.   I gain weight in Italy.

HOWARD.   Come with me.

PHYLLIS.   Why?

HOWARD.   We could be happy.

PHYLLIS.   What about Bishop?

HOWARD.   Leave him. *(Bishop's head turns at this.)* It'll just be us.

PHYLLIS.   No.

HOWARD.   Think about it. I have to go. Join me next week, please.

PHYLLIS.   I've been very stupid Howard.

HOWARD.   Think about it. *(Phyllis crosses and sits by Bishop. Howard addresses the audience.)* They called me in Italy to tell me the plane went down. I was relieved. And sorry. And sad and happy and guilty. I can't remember Bishop's voice anymore. When I close my eyes, I can see his face. But I can't make his voice in my head. *(Pam crosses the stage.)*

PAM.   It's five years, Howard.

HOWARD.   What?

PAM.   They're dead.

HOWARD. I suppose.

PAM. Howard?

HOWARD. Yes?

PAM. I'm pregnant. *(Pam is gone. Howard exits. Lights come up on Bishop and Phyllis. She reaches spastically for the sky. She seems shellshocked, he in control.)*

PHYLLIS. The sky.

BISHOP. What?

PHYLLIS. The sky. The sky — is — very blue.

BISHOP. Yeah so and.

PHYLLIS. Blue and bottomless.

BISHOP. It's up.

PHYLLIS. What?

BISHOP. It's up, asshole.

PHYLLIS. What is?

BISHOP. The sky is up, fucking dusthead.

PHYLLIS. Oh.

BISHOP. So, of course it's bottomless.

PHYLLIS. Oh?

BISHOP. If it had an end, it would be a top.

PHYLLIS. Oh.

BISHOP. Not a bottom.

PHYLLIS. Of course.

BISHOP. *(He starts doing push-ups.)* Fucking dusthead.

PHYLLIS. Of course. What are you doing?

BISHOP. Push-ups, crudbrain.

PHYLLIS. Oh.

BISHOP. What's it look like?

PHYLLIS. It looks like push-ups. Days. Years. Push-ups. You do push-ups. A sit-up would kill you. A squat-thrust would be too much —

BISHOP. Look at my body! My body is a fucking building! A cocksucking tower. My body is the fucking fabulous French Eiffel Tower!

PHYLLIS. It's very nice.

BISHOP. It's the ass-kicking pyramids.

PHYLLIS. What day is it?

BISHOP. Monday.

PHYLLIS. It was Monday yesterday.

BISHOP. It was fucking Sunday yesterday. Fucking dusthead.

PHYLLIS. No, no — I asked you what day it was yesterday and you said it was Monday.

BISHOP. Fuck you.

PHYLLIS. Didn't you?

BISHOP. It was Sunday so I said it was Sunday.

PHYLLIS. You always say it's Monday.

BISHOP. Crumbhead.

PHYLLIS. Maybe I only ask once a week.

BISHOP. Lintbrain.

PHYLLIS. Time flies.

BISHOP. Crudhead.

PHYLLIS. See that cloud?

BISHOP. Sandhead.

PHYLLIS. It looks like her.

BISHOP. Like who, trashhead?

PHYLLIS. Like her. Like Katharine Hepburn.

BISHOP. Garbagenoodle.

PHYLLIS. She looks beautiful. She looks young. I feel frumpish.

BISHOP. Christ.

PHYLLIS. I'm tired.

BISHOP. I'm hungry.

PHYLLIS. I want to sleep.

BISHOP. Cook something.

PHYLLIS. I'm sleepy.

BISHOP. Cook, slophead!

PHYLLIS. No.

BISHOP. Don't "no" me!!

PHYLLIS. Bishop!

BISHOP. Don't answer me!!

PHYLLIS. I'm sorry.

BISHOP. Muckbrain.

PHYLLIS. Bishop?

BISHOP. What is it?

PHYLLIS. No one is coming.

BISHOP. Shut up.

PHYLLIS. *(After a moment.)* Could you kill me?

BISHOP. I could.

PHYLLIS. Then do.

BISHOP. Shut up.

PHYLLIS. I do not want to go on. I just don't think I want to.

BISHOP. Turdhead.

PHYLLIS. Monday after Monday. After Monday.

BISHOP. Then it's Tuesday. If you want a Tuesday, it's fucking Tuesday. Are you happy? I make it Tuesday.

PHYLLIS. I want someone else.

BISHOP. If I say it's fucking Tuesday. It is.

PHYLLIS. My voice sounds very strange to me. It's been too long. It's been forever. Just air and space and Katharine Hepburn looking down at us. I want someone to take care of me.

BISHOP. I take care of you.

PHYLLIS. Thank you.

BISHOP. I catch things!

PHYLLIS. I know.

BISHOP. We eat!

PHYLLIS. We do.

BISHOP. So shut up.

PHYLLIS. I want someone to protect me.

BISHOP. I protect you.

PHYLLIS. I don't want to wait anymore. I've waited long enough. I'm all dressed up, on the stoop, waiting and waiting and no one is coming. I want to go inside. I want to give up. I want to lie down. No one is coming for us, Bishop.

BISHOP. They are too.

PHYLLIS. THEY ARE NOT!!! — And you can kill me. You can kill things. You can. I've seen you.

BISHOP. Shut up!!

PHYLLIS. I'VE SEEN YOU KILL THINGS! YOU KILL THEM WITH THE ROCKS AND THE BRANCHES AND YOUR HANDS, AND YOU CAN, AND YOU CAN KILL ME!! PLEASE!

BISHOP. SHUT UP!! *(He knocks her down, she may be crying.)*

PHYLLIS. I wish —

BISHOP. Always thinking of your fucking self.

PHYLLIS. I wish someone —

BISHOP. Who would I talk to?

PHYLLIS. I wish someone would —

BISHOP. Fucking monkeys?

PHYLLIS. I wish someone would hold me. I wish I had, I wish I was, I wish, I wish. I wish.

BISHOP. Be quiet. *(He approaches her. He puts his hand on her hair.)*

PHYLLIS. Bishop?

BISHOP. Be quiet.

PHYLLIS. Bishop. *(He places his hand on her breast and kisses her mouth.)* No.

BISHOP. Shut up.

PHYLLIS. No, no, no! Stop it!! Stop it!

BISHOP. SHUT UP! *(He yanks her head back and kisses her again. She struggles.)*

PHYLLIS. PLEASE!! GOD!! HELP!! THIS ISN'T WHAT I MEANT!!

BISHOP. SHUT UP!! SHUT UP!!! SHUT UP!!!

PHYLLIS. GOD HELP ME!!!! *(He forces her to the ground and tears at his clothes in a frenzy.)* GOD!! GOD!! HELP ME!! PLEASE!!! (Pam rises and walks down center, blocking our view of Phyllis and Bishop.)*

PAM. *(Out.)* There will now be a brief intermission. *(Blackout. We hear a song such as "Bali Ha'i."*)*

END OF ACT ONE

* See Special Note on Songs and Recordings on copyright page.

ACT TWO

Scene 1

The living room. Actually, the furniture is on the beach, arranged as if it were in a living room. There are two chairs, a sofa, a bar, and a television with its back to the audience. Pam is watching television.

PAM.   Howard! Howard! They're on again! They're showing it again! *(Out.)* I love CNN. *(To Howard.)* Howard! They're showing Phyllis and Bishop getting off the plane again! — *(Out.)* the same footage over and over. That Ted Turner — a genius. *(To Howard.)* Howard!
HOWARD.   *(Enters, tucking in his shirt.)* What?
PAM.   They were showing that clip again. Phyllis and Bishop getting off the plane.
HOWARD.   Oh, what time is it?
PAM.   Almost three.
HOWARD.   They should be here.
PAM.   Are you nervous?
HOWARD.   No. Yes. What time is it?
PAM.   It's almost three.
HOWARD.   They should be here.
PAM.   You said that.
HOWARD.   Did I?
PAM.   Do you want me to leave?
HOWARD.   Yes.
PAM.   Where would I go?
HOWARD.   No. Stay.
PAM.   You love me, Howard.
HOWARD.   What?
PAM.   Remember that. And our baby inside of me. We're going to have a whole new life together.
HOWARD.   Maybe you should go.
PAM.   I live here.

HOWARD. But I don't think she should walk in and find you.

PAM. We could say I'm the maid.

HOWARD. Yes.

PAM. And you could explain things to her gradually.

HOWARD. Do you have a uniform?

PAM. No.

HOWARD. Can you cook an egg?

PAM. No.

HOWARD. What if someone wants eggs?

PAM. Why would they want eggs?

HOWARD. What if they're hungry and they want some eggs?

PAM. You don't eat eggs. We don't have eggs.

HOWARD. You can't be the maid.

PAM. Maybe I should go.

HOWARD. Where will you go? Will you be all right? I'll take care of you. I'll support the baby. You won't have to worry.

PAM. I meant to the movies.

HOWARD. Oh.

PAM. Or for a walk. I meant for a little while.

HOWARD. Of course.

PAM. So that you could have some time alone with them. To talk with them. To explain what we've discussed. What we decided.

HOWARD. What we decided?

PAM. They can't stay here, Howard. I mean, they can stay here overnight, or through the weekend. But we agreed, they can't stay here. You have a new life now.

HOWARD. But I can't just throw them out. He's my wife and she's my son.

PAM. But we agreed.

HOWARD. What are you saying Pam?

PAM. I'll go out. You talk to them.

HOWARD. I think you should stay.

PAM. You do?

HOWARD. You're right. We have a life together and a baby

coming and I think we should face this together. It was over a long time ago with Phyllis and I'm sure if we present ourselves — I'm sure she's fine, I'm sure she's mature, I'm sure she's rational, I'm sure she's calm, I'm sure she's — *(Doorbell.)* Hide!!

PAM. What?!

HOWARD. It's them! Hide!

PAM. What? Where?

HOWARD. Get in the closet! Just get in the closet!

PAM. Howard! *(Howard shoves Pam into the closet. Phyllis and Bishop appear at the door.)*

HOWARD. Phyllis! Son!

BISHOP. *(To Phyllis.)* Go IN.

PHYLLIS. I don't want to.

BISHOP. GET IN THERE!

PHYLLIS. No.

HOWARD. Come in?

PHYLLIS. No thank you.

HOWARD. Pardon?

PHYLLIS. No thank you.

BISHOP. MOVE!

HOWARD. Won't you come in?

PHYLLIS. I don't think so. I like the hallway.

BISHOP. Shit.

HOWARD. I don't understand.

PHYLLIS. It's nice. The wallpaper is pretty. It's mint. I think I would describe this color as mint. I never noticed it before. It has a very delicate stripe.

HOWARD. You're not coming in?

PHYLLIS. Could you bring me some shoes? They gave me flats. I feel short.

HOWARD. Shoes?

PHYLLIS. Yes please.

BISHOP. We're late because the shithead kept making the taxi drive around the block.

HOWARD. I don't think you should call your mother shithead. I think it's disrespectful.

PHYLLIS. Shoes please?

HOWARD. Just a minute. *(He runs off.)*
BISHOP. Get in there!
PHYLLIS. I don't want to. Please don't make me. Please. I'll do anything. I don't want to go in.
BISHOP. It's our home, dirthead!
PHYLLIS. Can't we move? Get something smaller across town? A studio maybe? With a tub in the kitchen.
BISHOP. NO! Now go in.
PHYLLIS. You go in. I'll stay here.
BISHOP. You have to go in eventually.
PHYLLIS. No I don't. You can go in and slide food through the mail slot.
HOWARD. *(Re-enters carrying a pair of shoes.)* Here we go! Shoes!
PHYLLIS. Take them. *(Bishop takes the shoes from Howard and passes them to Phyllis, who puts them on her hands.)*
BISHOP. Here.
PHYLLIS. These shoes are beautiful.
HOWARD. Thank you.
PHYLLIS. They're too small. Do you have something in an eight?
HOWARD. An eight?
PHYLLIS. These aren't my shoes. These are a six. I'm an eight. These are sixes. Bishop, are these your shoes?
BISHOP. God!
PHYLLIS. Bishop, have you been wearing ladies' shoes? I should never have sent you to a private school. I don't mean to be judgmental —
BISHOP. THEY ARE NOT MY SHOES!
PHYLLIS. Oh.
HOWARD. Don't you like them?
PHYLLIS. Are you a transvestite now, Howard?
HOWARD. They're my mother's shoes.
PHYLLIS. Your mother died when you were five.
HOWARD. They're an heirloom.
PHYLLIS. That's touching.
HOWARD. Won't you come in now?
PHYLLIS. And they look right up-to-the-minute. Funny how

41

fashion repeats itself.

HOWARD. Someone will get off the elevator. Someone will see you.

BISHOP. I'm going in.

PHYLLIS. Bishop!!!

BISHOP. *(He rushes into the room and stands center.)* Look. Look, airbrain —

HOWARD. I don't think you should call your mother an airbrain.

BISHOP. Shut up. — Look. I'm in. I'm inside and nothing happened. It's fine. It's fucking fine. There's nothing to be afraid of. — What the fuck you staring at?

HOWARD. I don't understand.

BISHOP. The crudhead's afraid to come in —

HOWARD. I don't think you should call your mother a crudhead.

PHYLLIS. I'll never get out.

HOWARD. What?

PHYLLIS. If I come in. I'll never get out again. And the room doesn't look very big. And I don't recognize the furniture.

HOWARD. It's new.

PHYLLIS. Oh.

HOWARD. Don't you like it?

PHYLLIS. *(Waving at furniture.)* I don't even know it. How could I like it?

HOWARD. Bishop likes it. Don't you, Bishop?

BISHOP. I HATE IT!!!!

PHYLLIS. He forms opinions quickly.

BISHOP. IT'S UGLY!!!

PHYLLIS. Someone's getting off the elevator! Someone's coming! *(She runs into the room.)*

HOWARD. There.

PHYLLIS. I don't like it here! I don't like it. I want to go. This isn't my home. This isn't my furniture!

BISHOP. Get ahold of yourself, vomithead.

HOWARD. I don't think you should call your mother vomithead.

PHYLLIS. This isn't my living room. Everything's different!

This isn't my chair!

HOWARD.   It's new.

PHYLLIS.   I want my chair! Where's my chair!?

HOWARD.   It's gone. You like this one.

PHYLLIS.   I don't! It's strange. Ooh, ick, I hate this chair.

BISHOP.   The chair is fine, bilebrain.

HOWARD.   I don't think you should —

PHYLLIS.   I WANT MY OLD CHAIR!

HOWARD.   But.

BISHOP.   Get her old chair, for Christ's sake.

PHYLLIS.   I WANT IT. I WANT IT.

HOWARD.   I threw it out.

PHYLLIS.   WHY!!?

BISHOP.   *(Threatens.)* That was stupid.

HOWARD.   I redecorated. I just got some new furniture. That's all.

PHYLLIS.   This isn't my home. Where am I? My home has a wingback chair. Where am I?

HOWARD.   You are home.

PHYLLIS.   I don't think so.

BISHOP.   You shouldn'ta thrown it out, craphead.

HOWARD.   I don't think you should call me craphead —

BISHOP.   Shut up.

PHYLLIS.   Wherever I am. I want to leave. Can I leave here? Do you think we could go, Bishop?

BISHOP.   We just got here —

PHYLLIS.   But I don't like it.

HOWARD.   What's wrong with her?

BISHOP.   She's nuts, splitbrain —

HOWARD.   I don't think —

PHYLLIS.   *(Hiding her eyes with the shoes, she sinks to the ground.)* This is not my home.

BISHOP.   She's a dusthead.

PHYLLIS.   Is not. Is not. Is not.

BISHOP.   Ignore her.

PHYLLIS.   Is not. Is not. Is not.

BISHOP.   Yeah. She'll shut up.

HOWARD.   Maybe she should lie down.

BISHOP.   Do you want to lie down?

PHYLLIS.   My feet hurt.

HOWARD.   What does that mean?

BISHOP.   It means her feet hurt, phlegmhead.

HOWARD.   I don't think you should call me —

BISHOP.   Yeah, yeah, yeah.

PHYLLIS.   My feet hurt.

HOWARD.   Would you like to lie down?

PHYLLIS.   These shoes are pretty, but they're too small.

BISHOP.   She doesn't want to lie down.

PHYLLIS.   I think they're a six.

BISHOP.   Ignore her.

PHYLLIS.   I'm an eight.

HOWARD.   Ignore her?

PHYLLIS.   Do you have anything in an eight? A pump?

BISHOP.   She'll shut up. You'll shut up, won't you dusthead?

PHYLLIS.   Black crocodile, maybe?

HOWARD.   Well, sit down, son.

BISHOP.   You sit down.

HOWARD.   *(Sitting.)* All right.

PHYLLIS.   Do you have anything in patent leather?

HOWARD.   How are you son?

BISHOP.   Gee, I'm fine, thanks. And you?

HOWARD.   Good, good. I'm good.

BISHOP.   That's good.

HOWARD.   I'm fine.

PHYLLIS.   I'd like to see this in an eight.

HOWARD.   It's good to have you home.

BISHOP.   Mmmmmmmm.

HOWARD.   It's good to have you home.

BISHOP.   You said that.

HOWARD.   Oh. *(Reaching out to Bishop.)* Tell me. Was it terrible. Do you want to talk about it?

BISHOP.   Want to make a movie of it?

HOWARD.   Well, maybe.

BISHOP.   Fuck you.

HOWARD.   I don't think —

PHYLLIS.   *(Out.)* Excuse me, could someone help me?
HOWARD.   What?
PHYLLIS.   *(Out.)* Could someone — I'd like to try something on.
BISHOP.   Ignore her!!
PHYLLIS.   *(Out.)* Could someone help me?
HOWARD.   Well. I guess you're anxious to get back to school, back to your friends?
BISHOP.   What friends?
HOWARD.   Your little friends —
BISHOP.   I'm not going back.
HOWARD.   You have to go to school.
PHYLLIS.   *(To Howard.)* Could someone help me please?
HOWARD.   Everybody goes to school.
BISHOP.   Do you?
PHYLLIS.   *(Out.)* This is a terrible store.
HOWARD.   You used to like school.
PHYLLIS.   *(Out.)* The salespeople hate me.
HOWARD.   You used to enjoy it.
BISHOP.   That was then.
HOWARD.   Well, once you go back —
BISHOP.   I'M NOT GOING BACK!
PHYLLIS.   *(To Howard.)* Could someone please, please help me?
HOWARD.   You try it. You go back and give it a try.
PHYLLIS.   *(More desperate.)* Please, please, please!
BISHOP.   *(To Howard.)* Fuck you.
HOWARD.   Maybe not this week. You rest this week.
PHYLLIS.   Please, please, please!
HOWARD.   Maybe next week. You'll go back next week and you'll see you like it.
BISHOP.   It's summer! You asshole! It's fucking summer! What will I do at the fucking school when I get there! It's fucking summer!
HOWARD.   Well there is summer school!!! Maybe you've heard of summer school!!! It's school! And they have it in the summer!!
BISHOP.   Shut up!

HOWARD.   I don't mean to shout.

BISHOP.   Fuck you!

HOWARD.   I don't mean to lose my temper.

BISHOP.   Drop dead!

HOWARD.   I mean to be a good father!

PHYLLIS.   *(Out; breaking down.)* All I want — all I want to do, all I want to do is, I want to try, I want to try on some shoes! Shoes! Shoes. And no one will pay any, no one will wait, wait on me! I need some, some, no one will, will, will someone help me, help me, help me, help me —

HOWARD.   *(Going to her.)* Calm down Phyllis, calm down. It's all right. I'm here. I'm here.

BISHOP.   *(Almost chanting.)* DO NOT TOUCH HER! DO NOT TOUCH HER! DO NOT! DO YOU UNDERSTAND ME!!!? DO NOT!

PHYLLIS.   I —

BISHOP.   DO NOT! DO NOT! DO NOT! DO NOT! DO NOT! DO NOT! *(There is a blackout and Howard steps into a pool of light. As he speaks, the lights come up dimly behind him. We see Bishop dragging on a huge bag of shoes, mostly tattered-looking. Bishop and Phyllis arrange the shoes around her on the floor.)*

HOWARD.   *(Out.)* I don't know if Bishop went to school. About three days after he came back, he started leaving. Going out in the morning and coming back at night. I thought, if he went to school, if he saw people his own age, he would calm down. *(To Bishop.)* Are you going to school, Bishop?

BISHOP.   *(From his place by Phyllis.)* NO!

HOWARD.   Where are you going?

BISHOP.   NONE OF YOUR FUCKING BUSINESS!

HOWARD.   *(Out.)* We had what you might call a negative rapport. And Phyllis sat in the living room. Arranging her shoes. Breaking my heart. Occasionally, she made sense, but mostly, Bishop was right. It was best to ignore her. She slept on the floor of the living room and Pam came to me. Creeping past her. *(Pam enters and joins Howard in his pool of light. While they talk, we see, dimly, Bishop caressing, fondling and making love to Phyllis.)*

PAM.   It's long enough Howard.

HOWARD. What?

PAM. I can't go on like this.

HOWARD. Like what?

PAM. Living in the closet.

HOWARD. Oh.

PAM. With them here.

HOWARD. Be patient.

PAM. I need you Howard.

HOWARD. *(Out.)* I felt so guilty.

PAM. Send them away.

HOWARD. I feel so guilty.

PAM. You didn't do anything.

HOWARD. They need me.

PAM. She's insane.

HOWARD. She's confused.

PAM. He's dangerous.

HOWARD. He's highstrung.

PAM. They need help.

HOWARD. I'm his father.

PAM. Put them away.

HOWARD. You look very beautiful.

PAM. Howard. *(Pam leaves the light. The light behind Howard goes out so he is alone onstage.)*

HOWARD. *(Out.)* And Pam pushed me. And we made love. And in her breasts I forgot my savage son and my addled wife. Her skin is as white as beach sand, and I made circles around her nipples with my tongue. And in the darkness as I fucked her, as she panted, not to wake them, Bishop saw us. He watched from the hallway. He stared at the door. He stood in the dark. And I knew he was watching, and I pounded harder and she said I was a god. And I was trapped, unable to move in any direction. *(Howard exits. The lights come up on Phyllis playing with her shoes. Pam enters, now visibly pregnant. Some time has passed. She is dressed in a maid's uniform. She dusts.)*

PAM. 'Scuse me.

PHYLLIS. I was arranging my shoes.

PAM. I was going to dust in here.

PHYLLIS.   You can.

PAM.   *(Sarcastic.)* I won't disturb you?

PHYLLIS.   I am so disturbed already.

PAM.   It's a lot of shoes.

PHYLLIS.   None of them fit.

PAM.   Where do they come from?

PHYLLIS.   Shoe stores, I think.

PAM.   Oh.

PHYLLIS.   Or the garbage.

PAM.   Oh.

PHYLLIS.   Bishop brings them.

PAM.   Oh. That one's nice.

PHYLLIS.   You can have it.

PAM.   Well, thank you.

PHYLLIS.   I don't like it.

PAM.   Oh.

PHYLLIS.   And it has no mate.

PAM.   *(Dropping it.)* Well thank you anyway.

PHYLLIS.   I'm hungry.

PAM.   *(Miserable.)* Would you like me to get you something?

PHYLLIS.   You're a bad cook.

PAM.   I know.

PHYLLIS.   I feel like … eggs!

PAM.   What?

PHYLLIS.   I think I'd like some scrambled eggs.

PAM.   How about a sandwich?

PHYLLIS.   No. Eggs.

PAM.   Ice cream? We have ice cream.

PHYLLIS.   Why can't I have eggs?

PAM.   We don't have any eggs.

PHYLLIS.   *(Sinister.)* What kind of a maid are you?

PAM.   Howard doesn't eat eggs.

PHYLLIS.   I eat eggs.

PAM.   He doesn't like them.

PHYLLIS.   You are a terrible maid.

PAM.   I'm not the maid, Phyllis.

PHYLLIS.   *(Frightened.)* Are you her evil twin sister?

PAM.   No.

PHYLLIS.   Then you're the maid.

PAM.   No, no. I'm not.

PHYLLIS.   You look like the maid.

PAM.   I'm me. That's not what I mean.

PHYLLIS.   You're trying to drive me insane.

PAM.   I'm not.

PHYLLIS.   I think that's cruel.

PAM.   Listen to me.

PHYLLIS.   *(Out.)* And redundant.

PAM.   I'm not really a maid.

PHYLLIS.   Is this an argument for existentialism?

PAM.   No.

PHYLLIS.   If you're not the maid, then why are you dressed like that? Not that I don't like it. I do. It reminds me of my mother.

PAM.   Is she a maid?

PHYLLIS.   She's a waitress.

PAM.   I'm an actress.

PHYLLIS.   And you're preparing for a part?

PAM.   Not exactly.

PHYLLIS.   *(Giving up.)* Can't you just dust?

PAM.   I want to prepare you. I want you to understand.

PHYLLIS.   I don't think I want to.

PAM.   You know I'm going to have a baby.

PHYLLIS.   I just thought you had bad posture.

PAM.   And Howard is the baby's father.

PHYLLIS.   Howard? Howard, who?

PAM.   Your husband.

PHYLLIS.   He's sleeping with the maid?

PAM.   *(Losing her patience.)* Pay attention.

PHYLLIS.   How cliché.

PAM.   I wasn't a maid when I conceived!

PHYLLIS.   And he gave you a job. I think that's big-hearted.

PAM.   No Phyllis! Listen to me. Concentrate. Howard and I are in love. I'm not a maid. I've been pretending. He doesn't want to hurt you. He feels responsible for you. But time is passing and I think you're strong enough to see. To understand.

PHYLLIS.   Understand what?

PAM.   I plan to marry Howard. As soon as possible. I plan to marry him.

PHYLLIS.   I see.

PAM.   You do?

PHYLLIS.   Yes. That's why you never go home and you're here when I wake up and here when I fall asleep and why you creep past me at night and why you pretend there's a room where I know there's a closet.

PAM.   I hate that closet.

PHYLLIS.   It's a nice closet.

PAM.   Are you upset?

PHYLLIS.   No. What do I care if you like the closet?

PAM.   About Howard? About me?

PHYLLIS.   Oh. No.

PAM.   Really?

PHYLLIS.   Now I feel we can talk like friends. I felt class distinction prevented that when you were the maid.

PAM.   *(Out.)* There is dignity in any job well done.

PHYLLIS.   Howard plans to send me away then?

PAM.   He's afraid to.

PHYLLIS.   I know I should leave this room.

PAM.   He's not very strong.

PHYLLIS.   But I don't want to. I thought, when I was on the island, I thought all I wanted was walls. I thought I wanted a television. I thought I wanted cars and people. But when I try to get up, when I try to leave the room, I feel sick. Sometimes when no one's around, I try and I get really sick. It's not in my mind. I know you hate me.

PAM.   What?

PHYLLIS.   I know you hate that we're here. Please don't. I'm sorry. I'm sorry we came back. No one asked us.

PAM.   I'm sorry.

PHYLLIS.   No one ever asked me.

PAM.   Was it terrible?

PHYLLIS.   It wasn't that the sky went on forever, it was seeing the nature of things. The way things really are. It was being watched at night and seeing how the world really is.

PAM.   You don't have to talk about it. *(Bishop enters behind them, unnoticed.)*

PHYLLIS.   I was always the pretty one and my sister Marie was the smart one. And I was nice. Before I met Howard, I was. I was a nice person. I was pretty then. I thought that mattered.

PAM.   You're still pretty.

PHYLLIS.   No, my feet are too big. I'm an eight.

PAM.   I don't think so.

PHYLLIS.   No, I know I am. I've had my feet measured. I'm an eight.

PAM.   That's not what I meant.

PHYLLIS.   What did you mean? By what? When?

PAM.   Forget it.

PHYLLIS.   I'm confused. I want to leave the room. I do. I want to leave for Howard. Because he wants me to. And even though he wants me to for his own reasons, like he wants to sleep with the domestic help, I want to for him, because I don't hate him. Really. And I want to do it for me. Because I know people do. And I know that's what I should want. I should want to leave here and go shopping and have a life, and change my clothes — I think I've been wearing this dress forever — do I smell funny? — I know I should want these things, but I don't seem to be able to make myself. When I close my eyes all I see is the high high sky and the birds flying stupidly around Katharine Hepburn's face the way she looked in *Summertime* or *The Rainmaker* or *Sea of Grass*. And what scares me most of all — and this is really embarrassing — is I think I miss it.

PAM.   What?

PHYLLIS.   And that makes me want to just stop. And I cry. And Bishop comforts me. He protects me. And he holds me. When no one is looking. Late at night, when you're in your closet and Howard's in bed. Bishop comes to me and makes me feel all right for a minute. And I hold him against myself and pretend that she's watching and we're on the sand by the sea ... and it's really very beautiful — when we can pretend.

PAM.   Oh my god!

PHYLLIS.   What?

PAM.   I can't believe it! The two of you — that's terrible —

PHYLLIS.   You shouldn't judge.

PAM.   You poor —

PHYLLIS.   No, no, it's not his fault.

PAM.   We'll send him away.

PHYLLIS.   No.

PAM.   Howard doesn't know this, does he?

PHYLLIS.   Please —

PAM.   We'll send him away! He will.

PHYLLIS.   Don't tell him —

PAM.   Don't worry, Phyllis. He'll take care of it.

PHYLLIS.   He won't understand.

PAM.   I've got to go.

BISHOP.   *(Lunging at Pam with a knife.)* NO! *(Pam screams. Blackout.)*

Scene 2

The lights come up on Phyllis frantically packing shoes, trying to get all her shoes into a suitcase.

PHYLLIS.   Bishop! Bishop! *(Bishop enters, eating a sandwich and dragging what must obviously be Pam's leg.)*

BISHOP.   What?

PHYLLIS.   What are you doing?

BISHOP.   Eating. I'm hungry.

PHYLLIS.   Please. Don't get blood on the chair.

BISHOP.   Yeah yeah yeah.

PHYLLIS.   Help me.

BISHOP.   T'sorta dry. It could use some barbecue sauce. D'ya think we have any?

PHYLLIS.   I don't know. Help me. We've got to pack.

BISHOP.   Or soy sauce. Soy sauce would be good.

PHYLLIS.   What are you talking about?

BISHOP.   I'm talking about condiments!

PHYLLIS.   We've got to pack. We've got to get out of here.

BISHOP.   Why?
PHYLLIS.   You killed someone, Bishop.
BISHOP.   Yeah so and.
PHYLLIS.   Don't you understand?
BISHOP.   You want some?
PHYLLIS.   God no.
BISHOP.   *(Out.)* It's good but it's dry.
PHYLLIS.   Not "It's good," Bishop. "She's good."
BISHOP.   Maybe ketchup.
PHYLLIS.   You've committed murder!
BISHOP.   Or mayo.
PHYLLIS.   We have to get out of here.
BISHOP.   You overreact.
PHYLLIS.   Someone will find out! They'll find out and put
you away! We need disguises. Can you grow a mustache? Do
I have a wig? They'll catch you!
BISHOP.   Who?
PHYLLIS.   The police!
BISHOP.   Morons.
PHYLLIS.   You can't just murder people willy-nilly —
BISHOP.   I can.
PHYLLIS.   Where can we go? Have you ever been to Detroit?
BISHOP.   We don't have to.
PHYLLIS.   I'll dye my hair. Can you grow a beard?
BISHOP.   *(Threatening.)* Do you like your shoes?
PHYLLIS.   Help me think. Where can we hide?
BISHOP.   Do you?
PHYLLIS.   What's that got to do with anything?
BISHOP.   Just answer the fucking question!
PHYLLIS.   Yes.
BISHOP.   Where do you get them?
PHYLLIS.   You bring them to me.
BISHOP.   And where do you think I get 'em?
PHYLLIS.   I don't know.
BISHOP.   Where!
PHYLLIS.   Shoe stores?
BISHOP.   Wrong crapnoodle.
PHYLLIS.   The garbage?

BISHOP. Wrong, pissnoggin.

PHYLLIS. You steal them?

BISHOP. WRONG, sewageconk.

PHYLLIS. I don't want to know.

BISHOP. Why not?

PHYLLIS. I'd rather not —

BISHOP. People don't just give up their shoes!

PHYLLIS. *(Realizing.)* Oh my. Oh my God.

BISHOP. There are barefoot bodies all over town.

PHYLLIS. *(Frightened.)* Bishop, all these shoes?

BISHOP. I take care of you.

PHYLLIS. You did this?

BISHOP. For you.

PHYLLIS. You had no right.

BISHOP. Why not?

PHYLLIS. I don't know. It's not right. It's not moral.

BISHOP. *(Indicating the leg.)* With her it's moral, *(Indicating the shoes.)* with them, it's not?

PHYLLIS. *(A confidence.)* Well, I never really cared for her.

BISHOP. Some morals.

PHYLLIS. I feel sick.

BISHOP. Have a bromo.

PHYLLIS. We have to go. Now. Before your father comes home.

BISHOP. He can be dessert.

PHYLLIS. You shouldn't have killed her. I think he liked her. He's bound to notice.

BISHOP. Leave it to me, assholehead.

PHYLLIS. Don't call me that!

BISHOP. What?

PHYLLIS. What do you want to take?

BISHOP. You hate me. You wish I'd died in the plane crash.

PHYLLIS. Don't be absurd.

BISHOP. You hate me. I can tell!

PHYLLIS. You should not have murdered her. It showed poor judgment. You act in haste.

BISHOP. I had to!

PHYLLIS. Why?

BISHOP. You told her. She knew about us — she'd get them to put me away — you told her! It's your fault!

PHYLLIS. Don't blame me!

BISHOP. Why not? It's your fault!

PHYLLIS. You just wait until your father gets home —

BISHOP. You want them to catch me, admit it. You want to be alone with *him* again. You prefer him to me, don't you? It's obvious!

PHYLLIS. I didn't kill his little concubine, you did! It's fine as long as you do away with random strangers — you were fine when you couldn't be traced — but now you'll get caught. You never think ahead, that's your problem! There are repercussions.

BISHOP. I'M SORRY! ALL RIGHT! I'M SORRY! BUT IT'S DONE! WHAT DO YOU WANT ME TO DO ABOUT IT NOW!!?

PHYLLIS. *(Deadpan.)* Well, stop eating her for one thing.

BISHOP. I hate you.

PHYLLIS. Help me shut this —

HOWARD. *(Off-stage.)* I'm home!

PHYLLIS. Don't speak.

BISHOP. I'm not afraid of him.

PHYLLIS. Let me handle this. *(Hiding "the leg" in the sofa.)* I'll stall him. We'll leave tonight.

BISHOP. Yeah yeah yeah.

PHYLLIS. Please. *(She sits on her suitcase. Howard enters.)*

HOWARD. How is everyone?

PHYLLIS. Oh fine. Fine, fine, thank you.

HOWARD. And the shoes?

PHYLLIS. Oh, they're happy shoes.

HOWARD. Why the suitcase?

PHYLLIS. What suitcase?

HOWARD. That one.

PHYLLIS. Oh, this?

HOWARD. Planning a trip?

PHYLLIS. Redecorating. Like it?

HOWARD. Did you learn anything in school today, son?

BISHOP.   I don't go to school, you moron.

HOWARD.   I don't think you should call me a moron, Bishop. I think it's disrespectful. How can we be a family —

BISHOP.   I don't go to school, you dipshit.

HOWARD.   What's wrong with him?

PHYLLIS.   *(Shrugging.)* Kids today?

BISHOP.   Christ.

PHYLLIS.   I feel all in. Time for bed!

HOWARD.   Where's Pam?

PHYLLIS.   I'm pooped. Did we spring forward or fall back or something?

HOWARD.   Where is Pam?

PHYLLIS.   Who?

HOWARD.   Pam.

PHYLLIS.   *(Relocating onto the sofa in order to hide "the leg.")* I don't know anyone named Pam. Do you know a Pam, Bishop?

BISHOP.   You bet.

PHYLLIS.   I don't know who you mean.

HOWARD.   Pam. Pamela. The maid.

PHYLLIS.   Oh. Pam.

HOWARD.   Where is she?

PHYLLIS.   Out. Pam went out.

HOWARD.   Out where?

PHYLLIS.   Howard, I know I've been nutty and you've been unfaithful, but I feel all better now and I'd like to start over. Could we renew our vows?

HOWARD.   Out where? Where'd she go?

PHYLLIS.   Nevada. She went to Nevada.

HOWARD.   What?

PHYLLIS.   Yes. She wanted to play blackjack.

HOWARD.   Pam!

PHYLLIS.   She's gone. She wanted to play Big Six.

HOWARD.   God.

PHYLLIS.   She wanted to see Siegfried and Roy.

HOWARD.   Bishop!

BISHOP.   What?

HOWARD.   Where's Pam? *(Bishop belches.)*

PHYLLIS.   She wanted to see Elvis impersonators.

BISHOP.   How the fuck should I know?

PHYLLIS.   She left you to become Barry Manilow's maid.

HOWARD.   *(Losing his patience.)* What are you talking about!

PHYLLIS.   Barry Manilow. I love him. He writes the songs.

BISHOP.   Ignore her.

PHYLLIS.   It's hard to find loyal help. *(Bishop reaches into the sofa and pulls out a handful of "Pam.")*

HOWARD.   *(Disgusted.)* What is that?

PHYLLIS.   *(Rising.)* Let's remember happier times.

BISHOP.   Dinner. You want?

PHYLLIS.   Fresh air and sunshine. When Betty and Bud and Kitten were kids. Why, I remember once — oh, no, that's not us. That's *Father Knows Best.* Damn.

HOWARD.   *(Looks closer.)* What is that?!

BISHOP.   *(Revealing the leg.)* What's it look like?

HOWARD.   MY GOD!

PHYLLIS.   Anyone for Yahtzee?

BISHOP.   She's good but she's dry.

HOWARD.   What happened here?!

PHYLLIS.   Not to change the subject. But.

HOWARD.   *(Revolted.)* What the hell is that?

BISHOP.   *(Mock gee-whiz.)* Well, gosh Dad. I know it's the first time I brought a girl home, but I think it's love — I'd like ya ta meet Pam.

HOWARD.   *(Reaching out.)* Pam.

BISHOP.   I knew ya'd like her.

HOWARD.   Oh my God. Pam. *(Running off.)* Pam! Pam!

BISHOP.   If you want a leg there's more in the fridge.

HOWARD.   *(Returning.)* What are you?

BISHOP.   *(Yanking the leg.)* Starved!

HOWARD.   You did this!

BISHOP.   That's right.

HOWARD.   I'll kill you!

PHYLLIS.   Bishop, go to your room.

BISHOP.   Drop dead.

HOWARD.   *(Lunging at Bishop.)* I'LL KILL YOU!

BISHOP.   *(Pulling a knife.)* I don't think so.

HOWARD.   Try it! Try it, you little bastard!

PHYLLIS. I wouldn't taunt him dear. He's high-strung.

HOWARD. You're sick! You're insane!

PHYLLIS. Don't do it Bishop! I don't even like his shoes.

HOWARD. You're evil.

PHYLLIS. They're too clunky. I'd feel all masculine.

BISHOP. Shut up!

PHYLLIS. Howard, talk to your son. He shouldn't tell me to shut up.

HOWARD. Kill me! Kill me now, or I'll kill you!

PHYLLIS. I just said you should "talk" to him.

BISHOP. You never cared about me!

PHYLLIS. He has a point.

HOWARD. You killed someone — someone I cared about, cared for, someone I loved!!

BISHOP. I could never please you!

PHYLLIS. *(Momentarily affected by what she's heard.)* You loved her Howard?

HOWARD. Yes!

BISHOP. You see!

PHYLLIS. I knew, but I hoped —

HOWARD. I loved her!

PHYLLIS. Oh kill him, Bishop.

HOWARD. Phyllis!

PHYLLIS. Go ahead. You have Mother's permission.

HOWARD. What are you talking about?

PHYLLIS. *(Going to Bishop, cheerily.)* We're freaks and we belong together.

HOWARD. I'm calling the police.

PHYLLIS. *(To Bishop.)* Get him. *(Bishop lunges at Howard. There is a struggle. Out.)* Men being men.

HOWARD. *(Straddled by Bishop.)* Get off me! WHAT ARE YOU?

BISHOP. I could kill you like that and eat you for breakfast!

HOWARD. Please. You're sick. You should be in a hospital —

BISHOP. You just want to send me away! You're sorry I came back!

HOWARD. That's not true — I want to help you, I'll help

you!

BISHOP.   Lying motherfucker!

PHYLLIS.   Name-calling is a dirty business.

HOWARD.   You're my son. You need help!

PHYLLIS.   Someone's changed his tune.

BISHOP.   You don't get rid of me! I get rid of you!
WATCH!

HOWARD.   Phyllis!

PHYLLIS.   Yes dear?

HOWARD.   Help me! Stop him — call the police!

BISHOP.   YOU CAN'T GET RID OF ME! I'M YOUR
CHILD!

HOWARD.   CALL THEM!!

PHYLLIS.   *(After a moment of internal debate.)* No.

BISHOP.   YOU NEVER LIKED ME! YOU NEVER WANTED
ME!

HOWARD.   CALL THEM!

PHYLLIS.   I feel ... inert.

HOWARD.   Please Phyllis! I love you!

PHYLLIS.   Oh Howard. You love her, you love him, you love
me. You just love everyone when there's a knife at your
throat.

HOWARD.   HELP ME!!!

PHYLLIS.   *(Bored.)* Would you like a glass of water?

HOWARD.   Dear God oh god oh god —

BISHOP.   You should have killed me, you asshole! You
should have killed me years ago! When you had the chance,
when I was little — you didn't want me then — you don't
want me now — and it's not MY FAULT! IT'S YOURS! BUT
YOU COULDN'T! YOU'RE TOO SCREWED UP! YOU'RE
TOO FUCKED UP — WHAT'S RIGHT AND WHAT'S
MORAL AND YOU DIDN'T HAVE THE GUTS! BUT I'M
NOT YOU! I CAN DO IT! I CAN KILL THINGS! I CAN
KILL YOU!! AND IT FEELS TERRIFIC! IT FEELS LIKE RUN-
NING AND RUNNING AND GUNSHOTS IN MY HEAD!
AND THERE ARE BIRDS IN THE SKY, JUST LIKE YOU
AND I CAN CATCH THEM AND PULL THEM DOWN! AND
IT'S BETTER THAN FUCKING! WATCH! JUST WATCH!

JUST WATCH!!! *(He cuts Howard's throat. There is a long pause. Bishop collapses. Phyllis looks at him. Then at us. Then at Howard. Then at us again.)*

PHYLLIS.   Well … that was cleansing.

BISHOP.   Uh-huh.

PHYLLIS.   I feel good.

BISHOP.   *(At Howard.)* What a drip.

PHYLLIS.   You know, dear, I don't mean to criticize, but it would've been tidier to stab him in the chest.

BISHOP.   EVERYONE'S A MONDAY-MORNING QUARTER-BACK!!!

PHYLLIS.   Sorry. *(There is a pause.)* Bishop?

BISHOP.   What.

PHYLLIS.   What now?

BISHOP.   C'mere, slophead. *(She joins him.)* We'll go back.

PHYLLIS.   Back?

BISHOP.   Home.

PHYLLIS.   Tonight?

BISHOP.   Tomorrow. *(They look at each other and fall into a kiss, mutually. It is passionate.)* I'm starved. *(They look at Howard, then at each other and start to giggle.)* Don't eat the toes!

PHYLLIS.   I won't!

BISHOP.   *(Out.)* Toes are my favorite.

PHYLLIS.   *(Out.)* I like privates.

BISHOP.   That's my slop-head. — We'll go back and start over and always be together.

PHYLLIS.   I love you Bishop.

BISHOP.   Get the salt. *(Phyllis cheerily exits, and Bishop rises and addresses the audience.)* And the next thing I remember, I was someplace else completely. *(Blackout.)*

END OF ACT TWO

ACT THREE

A year later. A hospital. There are two areas set up on the sand. One is a consulting room: a desk with chair, and a chair for the patient. The other is Bishop's room: a cot and a small chest of drawers. Dr. Nestor is seated at the desk.

NESTOR. Send in Bishop Hogan. *(After a moment, Bishop enters.)* Hello.

BISHOP. Hello.

NESTOR. You are Bishop Hogan. Do you know who I am?

BISHOP. Do you know who *I* am?

NESTOR. I just said, you're Bishop Hogan. I am Dr. Nestor. *(Pause.)* Do you know why you're here?

BISHOP. Do you know why *you're* here?

NESTOR. I work here. I'm the new doctor.

BISHOP. *I'm* the new doctor.

NESTOR. Do you think you're a doctor?

BISHOP. Do you think *you're* a doctor?

NESTOR. I know I am.

BISHOP. I know *I* am.

NESTOR. I see.

BISHOP. I see.

NESTOR. I am Bishop Hogan. I am here because I murdered my parents. I killed my father and his mistress, and the next day, my mother. I am here because it was the judgment of the court that I was mentally ill at the time of these acts.

BISHOP. *I* am Bishop Hogan. *I* am here because I murdered my parents. *I* killed my father and his mistress, and the next day, my mother. *I* am here because it was the judgment of the court that I was mentally ill at the time of these acts.

NESTOR. I LIKE IT HERE.

BISHOP. I LIKE IT HERE.

NESTOR. I am all better and the psychological demons which tormented me have receded into the dark recesses of my unconscious.

BISHOP. Yeah yeah yeah, recesses, unconscious.

NESTOR. I thought you wanted to play a game.

BISHOP. Fuck you.

NESTOR. Fuck you.

BISHOP. What?

NESTOR. What?

BISHOP. Fuck off.

NESTOR. Fuck off.

BISHOP. You can't talk to me that way.

NESTOR. YOU CAN'T TALK TO ME THAT WAY!

BISHOP. I'm the patient. You're the doctor!

NESTOR. You're the doctor.

BISHOP. Fuck you!

NESTOR. FUCK YOU! *(Laughing.)* You see how irritating that can be.

BISHOP. *(Out.)* Dr. Nestor is eerily like my father.

NESTOR. Now. Shall we start over? *(Pause.)* Hello.

BISHOP. Hello.

NESTOR. Now, you're Bishop Hogan. Do you know who I am?

BISHOP. Fuck you.

NESTOR. That's better.

BISHOP. You're the new doctor?

NESTOR. Yes.

BISHOP. You remind me of my father.

NESTOR. It says here, you killed your father.

BISHOP. Yeah so and.

NESTOR. Do you remember that?

BISHOP. Like it was ten minutes ago.*

NESTOR. Why did you kill your father?

BISHOP. I was hungry.

NESTOR. Pardon me?

BISHOP. I was hungry and there were no spareribs in the kitchen.

NESTOR. Do you like Chinese food?

---

* Substitute actual time since Act Two killing of Howard.

BISHOP.   Comme ci, comme ça.

NESTOR.   You killed your father in a rage over an ill-stocked refrigerator?

BISHOP.   No. You moron.

NESTOR.   I don't think you should call me a moron, Bishop. I think that's disrespectful.

BISHOP.   I killed my father, to eat him. Didn't you read that thing?

NESTOR.   I meant to, but it got boring.

BISHOP.   Well, that's why I did it.

NESTOR.   All right. Why did you kill your mother?

BISHOP.   I didn't.

NESTOR.   I did read that far —

BISHOP.   I didn't kill my mother, you cocksucking, needlenosed dick!

NESTOR.   Do you feel hostile?

BISHOP.   Can we look at ink blots?

NESTOR.   You don't remember killing your mother?

BISHOP.   Since I didn't do it, why would I remember it?

NESTOR.   Maybe it slipped your mind?

BISHOP.   I remember things. I'm not insane.

NESTOR.   Then why are you here?

BISHOP.   You mean in the metaphysical sense?

NESTOR.   How did your mother die, if you didn't kill her?

BISHOP.   She didn't.

NESTOR.   It says here —

BISHOP.   I don't give a shit what it says there! I didn't write that! It's not true.

NESTOR.   So you think the other doctors are liars?

BISHOP.   Yes.

NESTOR.   And the judge?

BISHOP.   Yes!

NESTOR.   And the police?

BISHOP.   Yes!!

NESTOR.   And the courtroom stenographer?

BISHOP.   Yes!!!

NESTOR.   And the mortician?

BISHOP.   YES!!!

NESTOR.   And the undertaker?

BISHOP.   YES!!

NESTOR.   And me and Miss Fitch and the embalmer and the man who carved the headstone and the people from CNN and *Geraldo*?!

BISHOP.   YES! YES! YES! A BUNCH OF FILTHY-FUCKING-FREAKASSED LIARS! *(Phyllis enters. She looks composed and well-kept as she did at the start of the play.)*

PHYLLIS.   Bishop.

BISHOP.   *(Rushing to Phyllis.)* Mommy.

PHYLLIS.   Calm down, Bishop.

BISHOP.   They think you're dead.

PHYLLIS.   Don't be absurd — stand up straight.

BISHOP.   It's starting again. They're saying you're dead.

PHYLLIS.   Do I look dead?

BISHOP.   You're standing up.

PHYLLIS.   Do I sound dead?

BISHOP.   What do dead people sound like?

PHYLLIS.   Not like this.

BISHOP.   They say that I killed you.

PHYLLIS.   That's not true.

BISHOP.   I love you.

PHYLLIS.   Why would you kill me?

BISHOP.   I wouldn't.

PHYLLIS.   I know that.

BISHOP.   Why do they keep saying it then?

PHYLLIS.   They're incredibly stupid.

BISHOP.   All of them?

PHYLLIS.   Yes. They want to make you feel bad so they feel better themselves. They're insecure. They know they're stupid and they want to bolster their egos. They're jealous of us.

BISHOP.   What should I do?

PHYLLIS.   What would Katharine Hepburn do?

BISHOP.   Re-re-rely on her Yankee strength.

PHYLLIS.   That's right.

BISHOP.   Th-th-that's what I'll do then.

PHYLLIS.   And don't tell them anything. Don't give away your secrets. They'll use them against you. They'll judge you like God. Which they have no business doing.

BISHOP.   I love you Mommy.

PHYLLIS.   Why would you kill me? Don't chew gum. *(Phyllis and Bishop embrace. Popo enters wearing a bathrobe and sits on the cot.)*

NESTOR.   Send in Popo Martin, please. *(Popo rises and addresses the audience. She is* very *cheerful.)*

POPO.   I am Popo Martin. My friends call me Popo Martin. Dr. Nestor says I'm a paranoid schizophrenic. I think I have Marnie's disease. You know, like Tippi Hedren in that movie. When I see red, I see red! I mean, I have an episode. Although sometimes it happens when I don't see red. And sometimes I see red and it doesn't happen. I am the most popular girl in the hospital. I gets lots of visitors! I was a cheerleader. I'd do a cheer for you now, but I don't have my pompoms. All my teachers love me. The girls on the squad come to visit me every Sunday. The principal sent me a get-well note and the boys autographed a football. You can ask anyone in school about me, and they'd all say the same thing. Popo Martin is always cheerful. Popo Martin is a natural leader. Popo Martin looks on the bright side. Popo Martin has a smile on her lips and a kind word for a saddened stranger. Which is probably why everyone was so surprised when it happened. I tried to kill myself! I took thirty-five sleeping pills out of my mother's purse. I didn't want to smile anymore. My jaw hurts. And whistling gives me a headache. I want, more than anything, to wallow in a hopeless depression — but it just goes against my grain. So I tried to kill myself. That's why I'm here. *(Bishop and Phyllis have been watching her. Popo turns to Bishop and addresses him. As they speak, Phyllis recedes, but does not exit.)* I'm Popo Martin. You can call me Popo Martin.

BISHOP.   Yeah so and.

POPO.   *(Holding out a potholder.)* Look what I made!

BISHOP.   It's a square of fabric.

POPO.   *(Proud.)* It's a potholder!

BISHOP.   Mmmmmm.

POPO.   Don't you think it's beautiful?

BISHOP.   No.

POPO.   I do! I think it's the most beautiful one I've made yet! I've made thirty-seven potholders. Thirty-seven potholders and twenty-two ashtrays — which is odd, because they won't let you cook here, or smoke cigarettes. Do I seem cheerful to you?

BISHOP.   Grossly.

POPO.   I hate you.

BISHOP.   What are you doing here?

POPO.   I wanted to show you my potholder. I noticed you. You go after me, to see Dr. Nestor. *(She holds a potholder over each eye.)* Look, look! I'm Kitty Carlisle!

PHYLLIS.   She's an idiot Bishop.

BISHOP.   You're an idiot.

POPO.   You said something negative. So I didn't hear it. I tried to kill myself.

BISHOP.   Try, try again, I always say.

POPO.   Why are you here?

BISHOP.   This is my room.

POPO.   You look familiar. I know! You're that person who was on that desert island! You killed your parents! I saw you on *Geraldo*! You look thinner in person.

BISHOP.   That wasn't me.

POPO.   Can I have your autograph? Can I have your child? You're like a movie star. You look so much thinner. Wait till everyone hears that I know you! Could I kiss you?

PHYLLIS.   Bishop!

BISHOP.   No.

POPO.   Could I? You can put your hands on my breasts.

PHYLLIS.   Bishop!

POPO.   You can tie me up if you want. You can fuck me if you want!

PHYLLIS.   BISHOP!

POPO.   Bishop?

NESTOR.   Bishop!

BISHOP.   What?! *(Bishop leaves Popo, who returns to the cot. He joins Nestor at the desk. Phyllis follows.)*

NESTOR.   How are you today?

BISHOP.   You tell me.

NESTOR. You tell me.

BISHOP. Don't start.

NESTOR. Tell me about the island.

BISHOP. Well there was the Skipper and the Professor and Maryanne and a millionaire and his wife —

NESTOR. You were alone with your mother.

BISHOP. Yes.

NESTOR. How did you feel about that?

PHYLLIS. Tell him nothing.

NESTOR. Did you care for your mother?

BISHOP. You tell me —

NESTOR. I can't.

BISHOP. Too bad.

NESTOR. What was she like?

PHYLLIS. Was?

BISHOP. You mean "is" she like.

NESTOR. All right.

BISHOP. She's beautiful.

PHYLLIS. Thank you.

NESTOR. All right.

BISHOP. She loves me.

PHYLLIS. That's enough.

NESTOR. Do you love her?

PHYLLIS. *(Warning.)* Bishop.

BISHOP. Why?

NESTOR. Do you, believe, Bishop, that it's possible to love someone, to care for them and still hurt them?

BISHOP. I don't know.

NESTOR. You don't know?

BISHOP. It's too abstract.

POPO. *(On the cot, doodling his name.)* Bishop Hogan.

NESTOR. Do you think I want to hurt you?

PHYLLIS. Yes.

NESTOR. Do you think I care about you?

BISHOP. No.

NESTOR. Why not?

PHYLLIS. He's insane. You're fine.

BISHOP. Why would you?

67

NESTOR. Why wouldn't I?

BISHOP. I asked you first.

NESTOR. I asked you last.

BISHOP. You're insane.

NESTOR. You're a dick.

BISHOP. Fuckhead!

NESTOR. Asshole!

BISHOP. Dipshit!

NESTOR. Moron!

BISHOP. Spitbrain!

NESTOR. Crapnoodle!

PHYLLIS. This is absurd!

BISHOP. *(To Phyllis, who is stopping his fun.)* Leave me alone.

PHYLLIS. Bishop!

BISHOP. I'm sorry. *(To Nestor.)* Fuck you!

PHYLLIS. Atta boy!

POPO. *(Still on the cot, writing a letter.)* Dear Mom and Dad. Everything is great. I love it here. The food is really good and the weather is beautiful. The sun is always out and I can hear birds from the window of my room. The nurses are really nice and I am organizing a cheerleading squad of delusionary schizophrenics — but really they are just nice people who hear voices coming from inanimate objects. I think they do very well, considering the amount of phenobarbital they get pumped into them. I make really pretty potholders and ashtrays in workshop. I will make someone a great wife one day, assuming I cook and he smokes. On that subject, I have met the coolest guy. His name is Bishop Hogan. Maybe you heard of him. He's famous. He killed his parents. And some other people, I think. He's been on TV. But he's thinner in person. You'd like him. I can't wait for you to meet him. If you overlook the fact that he's delusionary, and that he butchered his parents and ate them, he's a fine catch. Love, Popo Martin.

NESTOR. Bishop.

BISHOP. What?

NESTOR. You killed a young woman.

BISHOP. Did I?

NESTOR. Didn't you?

BISHOP.   You tell me.

NESTOR.   You did.

BISHOP.   If you say so.

NESTOR.   I do.

BISHOP.   Fine.

NESTOR.   How did it feel?

BISHOP.   I don't remember.

NESTOR.   How it felt?

BISHOP.   Anything.

NESTOR.   What?

BISHOP.   I have amnesia.

NESTOR.   I see. And how did this happen?

BISHOP.   I guess I took a bump on the head.

NESTOR.   You guess?

BISHOP.   I can't remember.

NESTOR.   I see.

BISHOP.   Sorry.

NESTOR.   You remember this morning?

BISHOP.   Nope.

NESTOR.   Your mother?

BISHOP.   No.

NESTOR.   Your father?

BISHOP.   No!

NESTOR.   The island?

BISHOP.   NO!

NESTOR.   Your name?

BISHOP.   NO!

NESTOR.   CUT THE CRAP!

BISHOP.   What?

NESTOR.   You remember everything! You insignificant little slime! I know it! And you know it! You remember!

BISHOP.   I don't!

NESTOR.   Listen to me. You'll do as I say you little bastard. Or else! You will stay here in this hospital with paper slippers, soiled sheets and jello three times a day! You will stay here forever. We will pump you full of drugs and sit you in a yellow room with yellow walls and give you clay for ashtrays and yarn for placemats. And there you'll sit, till the days become years and your teeth fall out. And your hair falls out. And your muscles grow limp and you drool on yourself. And no one will visit you and no one will talk to you and no one will remember you and no one will care! And you'll really hear voices and you'll become old and your fingers will twist like the roots of a tree. And your organs will fail, one by one! And breathing's a chore! And you're just a body! Shuffling along! To no place at all! Every day! After day! After day! Until DEATH, FINALLY, MERCIFULLY, PATHETICALLY, PICKS YOU UP IN HER ARMS AND CARRIES YOU OUT OF HERE! NOW CUT THE CRAP!!!!

BISHOP.   Mommy!

PHYLLIS and POPO.   Bishop. *(Bishop starts to go to Phyllis but is cut off by Popo.)*

POPO.   I made this for you. *(She offers him a potholder.)*

BISHOP.   Leave me alone.

POPO.   I call it "Potholder Number 38."

BISHOP.   Put it away.

POPO.   It looks like Number 37, but it's not. It's better.

BISHOP.   Go away.

POPO.   You're welcome. *(She leaves him.)*

NESTOR.   Bishop!

BISHOP.   Go away!

NESTOR.   What happened to your mother?

BISHOP.   Nothing.

NESTOR.   She's alive?

BISHOP.   Yes!

NESTOR.   Where is she?

BISHOP.   Here!

NESTOR.   Right here?

BISHOP.   Yes!

NESTOR.   I don't see her!

BISHOP.   That's your problem!

NESTOR.   Look at me!

BISHOP.   What!

NESTOR.   You see her?!

BISHOP.   Yes!

NESTOR.   Where is she?!

BISHOP. HERE!
NESTOR. WHERE?
BISHOP. I DON'T KNOW!
NESTOR. Atta boy.
BISHOP. *(To Phyllis.)* Help me.
PHYLLIS and POPO. I'm here. *(Bishop and Phyllis embrace.)*
BISHOP. I couldn't find you.
PHYLLIS. Don't leave me.
POPO. I love you Bishop.
PHYLLIS. I need you.
BISHOP. I'm sorry.
POPO. I love you Bishop.
PHYLLIS. My feet hurt. I need new shoes.
POPO. I love you Bishop.
PHYLLIS. I need a place to sleep. I can't sleep on the beach with the clouds watching me. I need someone to protect me.
BISHOP. I'll protect you.
PHYLLIS. Tuck your shirt in.
POPO. I love you Bishop! *(Bishop hears Popo for the first time and moves to her.)*
BISHOP. What?
POPO. I think about you all the time. Dr. Nestor says I'm fixated. Dr. Nestor says I'm obsessing. Dr. Nestor says I'm off my nut!
BISHOP. He's right.
POPO. I dreamed about you last night.
BISHOP. Go back to your room.
POPO. I dreamed we were on a desert island.
PHYLLIS. Imagine.
BISHOP. Take a sleeping pill.
POPO. And I looked like Brooke Shields and you looked like Christopher Atkins.
BISHOP. Take a dozen.
NESTOR. Do you remember killing your mother?
POPO. And everything was idyllic.
BISHOP. Take a long walk off a short pier.
POPO. And the sun was very bright and our hair was blond.

NESTOR.   Bishop!

BISHOP.   Take a hike.

POPO.   And our bodies were perfect, and we went swimming.

BISHOP.   Take a rest.

POPO.   Naked.

NESTOR.   Do you?

BISHOP.   Take a leak.

POPO.   And we climbed out of the ocean, like Adam and Eve.

PHYLLIS.   What's the matter with her?

BISHOP.   She's obsessing.

POPO.   Like the birth of Venus.

PHYLLIS.   *(Out.)* God.

POPO.   And the water stuck to our skin, in droplets.

PHYLLIS.   Who cares?

POPO.   *(Calm.)* And the droplets reflected the sun and turned the rays of sunlight into prisms off our skin. And we stood on the beach, on the sand, nude with colors.

PHYLLIS.   Get rid of her.

POPO.   And we didn't speak.

PHYLLIS.   Bishop.

POPO.   Because we spoke with our arms and we spoke with our skin and we understood each other without any words. And you stood very close to me. And your breath was very warm on my face and the wind blew my hair and the waves filled my head.

PHYLLIS.   Don't touch her.

NESTOR.   *(To Phyllis.)* Leave him alone!

PHYLLIS.   SHUT UP!

POPO.   And I touched you. I put my hand on your shoulder.

PHYLLIS.   Don't let her.

POPO.   *(She does so.)* And your skin was soft and felt like singing to my fingers.

PHYLLIS.   Bishop.

BISHOP.   Leave me alone.

POPO.   *(As she continues, she becomes more and more relaxed, both*

72

in body and voice.) And the wind held my breasts and I kissed your neck. *(She does so.)* And it was sweet and smelled like flowers. *(Again.)* And I stopped hurting because I stopped smiling. *(Again.)* And I looked into your eyes. *(Again.)* And I saw my reflection

PHYLLIS. STOP THIS!

NESTOR. LEAVE HIM ALONE!

PHYLLIS. *(To Nestor.)* HE CANNOT DO THIS!

NESTOR. YOU'RE DEAD!

POPO. And you kissed me.

PHYLLIS. NO!

POPO. And you put your tongue in my mouth, and held my breasts, in the wind, your hands.

PHYLLIS. STOP IT!!

POPO. And you entered me, and the sun went behind a cloud and the shadows made dances on your chest —

PHYLLIS. STOP!

POPO. And it rained, on us, in the sand, on the beach, at the tide, in my arms, in your eyes, in my mouth, on my back, at your feet, by the sea, in my dream — *(Bishop and Popo embrace. Phyllis crosses to them.)*

PHYLLIS. Get rid of her Bishop!

NESTOR. Don't hear her Bishop.

PHYLLIS. Remember what it looks like!

NESTOR. *(To Bishop.)* Let her go!

PHYLLIS. Remember what it feels like!

POPO. I love you Bishop!

NESTOR. LET HER GO!

PHYLLIS. It feels like running and running Bishop — the taste of flesh in your mouth! Remember the taste! Remember the sounds! You said it Bishop! You can do it! Like gunshots in your head, better than fucking! Get rid of her! *(Bishop is holding Popo as if he might kiss her or kill her. Nestor removes his coat and becomes Howard.)*

POPO. I love you Bishop.

PHYLLIS. Kill her!

HOWARD. *(To Phyllis.)* STOP IT!

PHYLLIS.   What do you care?! You never wanted him to be-gin with!

HOWARD.   HE DOESN'T BELONG TO YOU!

PHYLLIS.   HE DOES!!

POPO.   I LOVE YOU!

PHYLLIS.   HE'S MINE!

HOWARD.   LOOK WHAT YOU DID!

PHYLLIS.   I DIDN'T DO ANYTHING —

POPO.   I LOVE YOU —

PHYLLIS.   YOU DID IT —

HOWARD.   HE KILLED YOU TOO —

PHYLLIS.   I LOVE HIM —

POPO.   I LOVE YOU —

BISHOP.   STOP IT! *(At this, Bishop pushes Popo off him. She removes her bathrobe, revealing Pam's costume. Nestor puts on his coat again and goes to his desk. Phyllis dishevels herself and sits where she sat before exiting at the end of Act Two. Pam and Phyllis revert to their Act Two personas.)* I killed her. I killed her. I did.

PAM.   *(After a long moment.)* I miss being alive.

PHYLLIS.   Bishop?

PAM.   *(Out.)* Go date married men.

BISHOP.   We ate my father through the night.

PHYLLIS.   I'm full.

PAM.   *(Out.)* Ick. *(Pam exits.)*

BISHOP.   And the sun came up. And we sat on the floor, the craphead and me.

PHYLLIS.   That was good. Do you want to watch TV?

BISHOP.   We have to go!

PHYLLIS.   Maybe something good is on the morning movie.

BISHOP.   We have to get out of here. You said it yourself.

PHYLLIS.   Maybe *African Queen* —

BISHOP.   Someone'll find us.

PHYLLIS.   Or *Philadelphia Story* or *Adam's Rib* —

BISHOP.   Someone will find them!

PHYLLIS.   *(Growing desperation.)* Or *Break of Hearts!* Or *Morning Glory!*

BISHOP.   You know we can't stay here!

PHYLLIS.   I could miss *The Lion in Winter* — Or *Christopher Strong!* Or *Woman of the Year!*
BISHOP.   We have to go back!
NESTOR.   She wouldn't cooperate?
BISHOP.   *(To Nestor.)* I didn't understand.
PHYLLIS.   We could play with my shoes?
BISHOP.   We can bring your shoes.
PHYLLIS.   It's a lot. I can't carry them all.
BISHOP.   I'll carry half.
PHYLLIS.   I want to see *Bringing Up Baby!*
BISHOP.   They'll find them. They'll catch us.
PHYLLIS.   Who?
BISHOP.   The police.
PHYLLIS.   I thought they were morons?
BISHOP.   *(Forceful.)* People are up. We have to go.
PHYLLIS.   I can't.
BISHOP.   Why not?
PHYLLIS.   I'm afraid.
BISHOP.   Of what?
PHYLLIS.   *(After a moment.)* You of course.
BISHOP.   I protect you.
PHYLLIS.   And ...
BISHOP.   What?
PHYLLIS.   You kill people.
BISHOP.   But I love you.
PHYLLIS.   So?
BISHOP.   *(To Nestor.)* She wouldn't come.
NESTOR.   And then?
BISHOP.   *(To Phyllis.)* Do you want to go to prison?
PHYLLIS.   No.
BISHOP.   You will. They'll lock you away and never let you out.
PHYLLIS.   But I didn't do anything wrong.
BISHOP.   They don't care. Everyone is guilty and they'll put you away.
PHYLLIS.   What's on TV?
BISHOP.   You've got to come.

PHYLLIS.   Don't make me.

BISHOP.   I won't leave you.

NESTOR.   Why not?

BISHOP.   I love her!

PHYLLIS.   You have to.

BISHOP.   I do what I want!

PHYLLIS.   You have to go.

BISHOP.   I'll stay with you.

PHYLLIS.   You'll get on my nerves.

BISHOP.   I'll be quiet.

PHYLLIS.   No. No. Bishop. You go. You go without me. You'll kill me someday, if I come.

BISHOP.   Maybe not.

PHYLLIS.   So kill me now. I'm tired.

BISHOP.   What?

PHYLLIS.   Kill me now.

NESTOR.   She asked you?

BISHOP.   *(To Nestor.)* SHUT UP!

PHYLLIS.   *(Positive; with love.)* We've done such things.

BISHOP.   I don't understand.

PHYLLIS.   I can't go on with you and don't want to without you. Please.

BISHOP.   You hate me. You wish I was dead.

PHYLLIS.   No. I love you. But see what I made.

BISHOP.   I can't.

PHYLLIS.   You can. You said it. It feels wonderful. It feels like running and running.

BISHOP.   Don't make me.

PHYLLIS.   Make me proud. Please, Bishop. *(Bishop and Phyllis embrace.)*

BISHOP.   I love you, Phyllis.

PHYLLIS.   I love you, Bishop. *(They kiss. It is long and romantic. As they kiss, he lowers her to the ground; there is no overt act of violence, but she is dead. Bishop rises and addresses the audience.)*

BISHOP.   I am Bishop Hogan, that is my name, I am not a deacon of the church. I killed my father and his mistress and the next day, my mother, whom I loved.... It was the

76

judgment of the court that I was mentally ill at the time of these acts.... And it was my mother's fault. And my father's. And my own. Because I am, what I create: And I understand that I must stay awake all the time, because when I sleep, when I shut my eyes, the monkeys come again. And it is no one's fault. It is the nature of the monkeys.

END OF PLAY

PROPERTY LIST

ACT ONE

ONSTAGE:
Flight bag (PHYLLIS) with lipstick, compact, and butcher's knife

OFF-STAGE:
Two cigars (BISHOP)
Cigar (HOWARD)
Champagne bottle (HOWARD)
Two champagne glasses (HOWARD)
Severed Nun's arm, still clutching rosary beads (BISHOP)
Severed man's leg (BISHOP)
Baby in blanket, with false stomach and edible innards (PHYLLIS)
Book (HOWARD)
Second severed man's leg, with edible innards (PHYLLIS)
Pill bottle, with pills (PAM)

ACT TWO

ONSTAGE:
Remote control

OFF-STAGE:
One pair of shoes, size six (HOWARD)
Suitcase filled with dozens of pairs of shoes (BISHOP)
Feather duster (PAM)
Knife (BISHOP)
Severed woman's leg, dressed as Pam, with edible innards (BISHOP)
Sandwich, with hand sticking out (BISHOP)
Tennis racquet (HOWARD)

ACT THREE

ONSTAGE:
Notebook, or medical chart
Giant pencil (POPO)
Oversized pad of paper (POPO)

OFF-STAGE:
Three potholders (POPO)
Stuffed animal, Snoopy (POPO)
Cigarette (PHYLLIS)
Lighter (PHYLLIS)
Pad of paper (BISHOP)
Pencil or pen (BISHOP)

COSTUME PLOT

ACT ONE

PHYLLIS
Mint green traveling suit, jacket and dress
Three-strand pearl necklace
Sunglasses
Stockings (natural)
Pearl earrings
Bone pumps
Patterned scarf
Second traveling suit, identical (distressed)
Natural stockings with runs and blood stains
Dress from traveling suit (very distressed)

BISHOP
Oversized school uniform:
    navy blue blazer with brass buttons and crest
    white oxford cloth shirt
    striped, red tie
    chinos
    white socks
    brown belt
    brown loafers
    horn-rimmed glasses
Snug school uniform:
    navy blue blazer with brass buttons and crest (distressed)
    white oxford cloth shirt (distressed)
    chinos, cut-off (distressed)
Blood-stained loin cloth
Necklace made from bones and shells

HOWARD
Tuxedo pants
Smoking jacket

Formal shirt
Bow tie
Black socks
Black dress shoes
Black suspenders
Tuxedo jacket
Brown dress pants
Brown woven belt
Chartreuse blazer
Baseball cap
Cream polo shirt
Navy blue socks
Sneakers
Green cardigan
Navy blue trousers
Khaki blazer
Brown and navy scarf
Blue shirt
Patterned band-collar shirt
Patterned sport coat

PAM
Cocktail dress, silver mini
Silver platform shoes
Silver bracelet
Silver earrings
Animal print pants
Silver bra-top
Sheer over-blouse
Black platform shoes
Black bracelet
Navy blue stretch bell-bottom pants
Hot-pink midriff blouse
Navy blue platform shoes
Navy blue earrings

ACT TWO

HOWARD
Brown pants
Natural silk blazer
Patterned shirt
Brown woven belt
Brown shoes
Tennis shorts
Tennis shirt
Wrist bands
White socks
Sneakers

PAM
Patterned, sheer blouse
Silver bra-top
Black stretch, bell-bottom pants
Black platform shoes
Caramel silk bathrobe
Pregnancy pad
Maid's uniform: black dress, apron, white hose, black shoes

BISHOP
Yellow slicker
Navy blue chinos
Patterned shirt
White socks
Brown shoes
Striped wind-breaker (distressed)
Navy blue chinos (distressed)
T-shirt (distressed)

PHYLLIS
Same as ACT ONE (Mint green dress, very distressed, no
    stocking or jewelry)
Add black flat shoes

ACT THREE

DR. NESTOR
White lab coat
Brown pants
Brown socks
Brown shoes
Glasses
(Under lab coat, Howard's cardigan and polo shirt)

BISHOP
Cream, band collar shirt
Cream draw string pants
Cream socks
Sneakers

PHYLLIS
Same as ACT ONE
(Mint green traveling suit, restore stockings and accessories)

POPO
Pink Bathrobe
Pink fuzzy slippers
Pink hair clips
(Under robe, Pam's silver bra-top)

SOUND EFFECTS

Doorbell

NEW
PLAYS

THE AFRICAN COMPANY PRESENTS
RICHARD III
by Carlyle Brown

EDWARD ALBEE'S
FRAGMENTS and THE MARRIAGE PLAY

IMAGINARY LIFE
by Peter Parnell

MIXED EMOTIONS
by Richard Baer

THE SWAN
by Elizabeth Egloff

Write for information as to
availability
DRAMATISTS PLAY SERVICE, Inc.
440 Park Avenue South   New York, N.Y. 10016

NEW
PLAYS

THE LIGHTS
by Howard Korder

THE TRIUMPH OF LOVE
by James Magruder

LATER LIFE
by A.R. Gurney

THE LOMAN FAMILY PICNIC
by Donald Margulies

A PERFECT GANESH
by Terrence McNally

SPAIN
by Romulus Linney

Write for information as to
availability
DRAMATISTS PLAY SERVICE, Inc.
440 Park Avenue South   New York, N.Y. 10016

NEW
PLAYS

LONELY PLANET
by Steven Dietz

THE AMERICA PLAY
by Suzan-Lori Parks

THE FOURTH WALL
by A.R. Gurney

JULIE JOHNSON
by Wendy Hammond

FOUR DOGS AND A BONE
by John Patrick Shanley

DESDEMONA, A PLAY ABOUT A HANDKERCHIEF
by Paula Vogel

Write for information as to availability
DRAMATISTS PLAY SERVICE, Inc.
440 Park Avenue South   New York, N.Y. 10016